Greater Than a Tourist Book Series
Reviews from Readers

I think the series is wonderful and beneficial for tourists to get information before visiting the city.

-Seckin Zumbul, Izmir Turkey

I am a world traveler who has read many trip guides but this one really made a difference for me. I would call it a heartfelt creation of a local guide expert instead of just a guide.

-Susy, Isla Holbox, Mexico

New to the area like me, this is a must have!

-Joe, Bloomington, USA

This is a good series that gets down to it when looking for things to do at your destination without having to read a novel for just a few ideas.

-Rachel, Monterey, USA

Good information to have to plan my trip to this destination.

-Pennie Farrell, Mexico

Great ideas for a port day.

-Mary Martin USA

Aptly titled, you won't just be a tourist after reading this book. You'll be greater than a tourist!

-Alan Warner, Grand Rapids, USA

Even though I only have three days to spend in San Miguel in an upcoming visit, I will use the author's suggestions to guide some of my time there. An easy read - with chapters named to guide me in directions I want to go.

-Robert Catapano, USA

Great insights from a local perspective! Useful information and a very good value!

-Sarah, USA

This series provides an in-depth experience through the eyes of a local. Reading these series will help you to travel the city in with confidence and it'll make your journey a unique one.

-Andrew Teoh, Ipoh, Malaysia

GREATER THAN A TOURIST- BERNESE OBERLAND SWITZERLAND

50 Travel Tips from a Local

Natacha Müller

The statements in this book are of the authors and may not be the views of
CZYK Publishing or Greater Than a Tourist.

Cover designed by: Ivana Stamenkovic
Cover Image:
https://pixabay.com/photos/gondolas-switzerland-niederhorn-2066932/
https://pixabay.com/photos/bachalpsee-bernese-horns-wetterhorn-487213/

CZYK Publishing Since 2011.

Greater Than a Tourist
Visit our website at GreaterThanaTourist.com

Lock Haven, PA
All rights reserved.

ISBN: 9781091968318

>TOURIST

50 TRAVEL TIPS FROM A LOCAL

BOOK DESCRIPTION

Are you excited about planning your next trip?

Do you want to try something new?

Would you like some guidance from a local?

If you answered yes to any of these questions, then this Greater Than a Tourist book is for you.

Greater Than a Tourist - Bernese Oberland/Switzerland by Natacha Müller offers the inside scoop on Switzerland's picturesque Bernese Oberland. Most travel books tell you how to travel like a tourist. Although there is nothing wrong with that, as part of the Greater Than a Tourist series, this book will give you travel tips from someone who has lived at your next travel destination.

In these pages, you will discover advice that will help you throughout your stay. This book will not tell you exact addresses or store hours but instead will give you excitement and knowledge from a local that you may not find in other smaller print travel books.

Travel like a local. Slow down, stay in one place, and get to know the people and culture. By the time you finish this book, you will be eager and prepared to travel to your next destination.

Inside this travel guide book you will find:

- Insider tips from a local.

- Packing and planning list.

- List of travel questions to ask yourself or others while traveling.

- A place to write your travel bucket list.

OUR STORY

Traveling is a passion of the "Greater than a Tourist" series creator. Lisa studied abroad in college, and for their honeymoon Lisa and her husband toured Europe. During her travels to Malta, an older man tried to give her some advice based on his own experience living on the island since he was a young boy. She was not sure if she should talk to the stranger but was interested in his advice. When traveling to some places she was wary to talk to locals because she was afraid that they weren't being genuine. Through her travels, Lisa learned how much locals had to share with tourists. Lisa created the *Greater Than a Tourist* book series to help connect people with locals. A topic that locals are very passionate about sharing.

TABLE OF CONTENTS

DEDICATION

To Simon, who always believed I could be a writer.
And to Julia, my soul sister.

ABOUT THE AUTHOR

Natacha grew up in a little village on Lake Thun. Ever since she was a child, she's loved the idea of traveling the world, exploring other countries, and learning more about foreign cultures. After her three-year commercial apprenticeship, she decided to combine her love of travel with her passion for helping people by volunteering in Fiji. She took on jobs in Panama and Costa Rica before working as a flight attendant for Switzerland's national airline. For three years, Natacha's jet-set lifestyle helped her discover destinations all over the globe. The more places she explored, the more she realized how uniquely beautiful the region she was lucky enough to grow up in really is.

HOW TO USE THIS BOOK

The *Greater Than a Tourist* book series was written by someone who has lived in an area for over three months. The goal of this book is to help travelers either dream or experience different locations by providing opinions from a local. The author has made suggestions based on their own experiences. Please check before traveling to the area in case the suggested places are unavailable.

Travel Advisories: As a first step in planning any trip abroad, check the Travel Advisories for your intended destination.
https://travel.state.gov/content/travel/en/traveladvisories/traveladvisories.html

FROM THE PUBLISHER

Traveling can be one of the most important parts of a person's life. The anticipation and memories that you have are some of the best. As a publisher of the Greater Than a Tourist book series, as well as the popular *50 Things to Know* book series, we strive to help you learn about new places, spark your imagination, and inspire you. Wherever you are and whatever you do I wish you safe, fun, and inspiring travel.

Lisa Rusczyk Ed. D.
CZYK Publishing

WELCOME TO
> TOURIST

*'Blessed are the curious for they
shall have adventures.'*

– Lovelle Drachman

Even though Switzerland is a small country, it's
packed with amazing adventures. There are so many
mountains to hike up, lakes to jump in, and areas to
explore that planning an itinerary can cause quite the
headache! Luckily, there's a region in the heart of this
beautiful country where you'll find the very best of
Switzerland. Welcome to my home region, the
Bernese Oberland.

In this guide book, I'll show you how to find the
best of the Bernese Oberland, including crystal-clear
lakes, cute alpine villages, and snowy mountains. No
other region in Switzerland can compete with what's
on offer here.

Most tourists only scratch the surface of all the
incredible things to do in this region. I want to use my
insider knowledge to help you experience my home
area like a local.

1. ABOUT SWITZERLAND

So, you're thinking about visiting the Bernese Oberland. Fantastic choice! I assume you still aren't sure where to go in a region with so much to offer. No problem, as you're currently holding the key to a perfect vacation in the Bernese Oberland. I'm here to take the stress out of planning the perfect trip. But before we dive into everything you can do, see, and eat in this beautiful region, you need to know a little bit about Switzerland as we're way more than just banks, watches, and cheese.

Switzerland lies in the very heart of Europe and is surrounded by five countries: France, Italy, Austria, Liechtenstein, and Germany. We're not to be confused with Sweden, an equally gorgeous country, which is a lot closer to the Arctic Circle than we are. People constantly (and annoyingly!) confuse the two nations.

Bern, not Zurich or Geneva, is our capital, and we have four national languages: German, French, Italian, and Romansh. 63% of our population speak German. French is spoken by 23% of us and mostly by those in the west where Switzerland borders

France. You can find the 8% that speak Italian in the canton of Ticino, which borders Italy. Romansh is only spoken by less than 1% of the whole population, but it's still considered a national language. Hardly any of us can speak all four - hats off to those who can. It's quite common to know two or three, though. I, myself, speak three (German, French, and Italian). But don't worry: Nobody expects you to fluently speak any of these languages when you come to Switzerland. Almost everyone here speaks excellent English, so communication with the locals shouldn't be a problem.

Switzerland has 26 cantons, but sometimes you'll read we have 23. This is because six of our cantons are half-cantons. When you come across someone or some document speaking of 23 cantons, it's because they've counted half-cantons (such as Obwalden and Nidwalden) as one, not two.

The Bernese Oberland (or the Berner Oberland as we locals call it) is a region that lies in the heart of the Bern canton. The most central town in the region is the ever-popular Interlaken. It's very easy to visit all the main sights, secret spots, and activities from here. If you open a map of the Bernese Oberland, you'll see that Interlaken is perched between Lake Thun and Lake Brienz. Ideally situated between the mountains and the lakes, Interlaken and the surrounding villages are the perfect vacation base.

Without further ado, let's start planning your trip to the Bernese Oberland, beginning with the best time to visit this beautiful region.

2. BEST TIME TO VISIT

If you're like me, the first thing you'll google when planning to go somewhere is the best time to visit. I'm usually very disappointed when I read it's super rainy or way too hot when I would've liked to travel. I'm here to deliver some good news: There's no bad time to visit the Bernese Oberland.

Summer's perfect for those who want to take a dip in our numerous lakes while spring's ready-made for hikers of all ability. In our crisp fall, the region's woodland turns shades of red and yellow while the winter months transform the area into one big snowy wonderland.

Most people think it's always cold in Switzerland (probably because they confuse us with Sweden), but I can assure you that it gets pretty hot in summer. Our average temperature in summer is around 75° Fahrenheit/24°Celsius, but it can reach 102° Fahrenheit/39°Celsius. In winter, the temperature in the valleys drops as far as 14° Fahrenheit/-10° Celsius, and it gets even colder up in the mountains.

3. WHAT TO PACK

I've spent the last few years jetting around the world, so I know exactly what it feels like when you finally arrive at your destination and think: 'Why did I even take this with me?' or 'why have I left that at home?'

To make sure this doesn't happen to you, I've compiled a little list of what's helpful to have when you visit the Bernese Oberland. Apart from the obvious, some items simply shouldn't be left at home.

You're definitely going to need all your camera gear. There's going to be photo opportunities wherever you go, so pack whatever you've got. It doesn't matter if that's just your smartphone - it'll still capture great shots.

Hiking boots should also find a place in your suitcase. You don't have to be a professional hiker to wear them. They're just ready-made for mountain terrain and much more comfortable on a long hike than regular sneakers.

Sunscreen and sunglasses are not only summer must-haves, as they'll also shield you from the alpine sun in the mountains. It goes without saying that if you happen to come here in winter, make sure you have all the warm winter essentials (gloves, hats, etc.). If you don't have any of those at home, there's plenty of shops here that sell cold weather gear. Warm boots will make cold winter nights a little less freezing. My personal tip: Make sure you get these boots a size bigger so you can wear cozy socks. They're a lifesaver! If you want to go skiing, sledding, or any of the many other snow-related activities, you should pack thermal underwear. They'll keep you warm throughout the day. The brand I've worn since I was a little kid is Odlo.

Another thing you need to know is that Swiss sockets are a bit strange. Even if you're from Germany (only a few hours away) some of your plugs won't fit. Make sure to pack the right adaptor. We have type J and type C.

You might have already realized, but we do things a little bit differently here. So just a little heads up if you have an EU sim card, there will be roaming charges for you in Switzerland as we're famously not in the EU, despite being right in the middle of Europe.

My last piece of advice is not something you necessarily have to pack but rather download onto your phone. It's always super handy to have a currency converter with you wherever you go. There's nothing more annoying than having to stand around in a store trying to calculate the conversion in your head. This will save you a lot of time - and potentially money! For the ones curious about mountains, there's an app for that too. It's called PeakFinder. Simply hold your phone against the mountain vista you'd like to know more about and the app will tell you all about it. Brilliant, isn't it?

4. HOW TO GET HERE

When you come to our beautiful country, chances are you're either flying into Zurich or Geneva Airport. They're our two biggest airports. The closest airport to the Bernese Oberland is Bern Belp Airport. However, not many planes fly directly to Bern, so I'm going to focus on Zurich and Geneva as they service the most international flights.

By car

If you rent a car at Zurich Airport, there are two ways to get to the Bernese Oberland. The quicker and more scenic route lasts about 1.5 hours and takes you to Interlaken via Lucerne and the Brünig mountain pass. Route number two is a bit less scenic as it sticks to the highway, but it avoids windy mountain roads. It goes to Bern and Thun and takes a little over 2 hours to arrive in Interlaken. It takes around 2.5 to 3 hours to drive here from Geneva, and you'll drive mostly on the highway past Lausanne, Yverdon, and Bern.

By train

Unlike most countries, the best way to get around Switzerland is by public transport. Our trains, buses, and trams are excellent, so getting to the Bernese

Oberland is pretty easy. If you're coming from Zurich, there are trains to Bern almost every 30 minutes, and they last about an hour. From Geneva, it takes around 2 hours to get to Bern, and trains leave every half an hour as well. Once you arrive in Bern, the Bernese Oberland is just around the corner. You just need to hop on another 40-50 minute scenic train ride that glides through our stunning landscape.

As mentioned before, Interlaken's the most central town in the Bernese Oberland. Before coming here, you need to know that Interlaken has two train stations. Interlaken West is the smaller of the two, but closer to the heart of the town. The big shopping street starts right at the end of this station, and most of my favorite cafés are in that area as well. The big bus station in Interlaken West will take you to places on Lake Thun, such as Spiez and Thun. It also runs bus services to the towns surrounding Interlaken, including Matten, Wilderswil, and Unterseen. Interlaken Ost, on the other hand, connects Interlaken with the mountains, towns, and villages on Lake Brienz. Buses go to villages such as Bönigen, Iseltwald, and Ringgenberg and trains venture to Grindelwald, Lauterbrunnen, and even Lucerne. Having two stations can sometimes be confusing though. I remember trying to meet some friends at a station and forgot to mention which one, and we ended up at different ones. So, before you hastily book a ticket somewhere, make sure to check which station your train is departing from.

Top tip: The SBB app (with its bright red icon) will tell you exactly when trains depart, where they stop, and when they arrive. You can even buy tickets directly on the app. This will save you from trying to figure out strange foreign train timetables, which are hung up at the stations. Just type in where you are and where you want to go, and the app will tell you when your train leaves.

5. HOW TO GET AROUND

Getting around Switzerland is super easy compared to some other countries. I remember having a hard time figuring out the NYC subway, and don't even get me started on the Beijing underground! Figuring out the Swiss transport system is a breeze in comparison. Like I said previously, the SBB app is your new best friend. Even if you're in the remotest village, the app will find a bus that takes you where you want to go. SBB CFF FFS is the national train company, but the app also covers buses and trams. If you're wondering what SBB means - it's Schweizerische Bundesbahnen, which translates to Swiss Federal Railways. CFF and FFS are just the French and Italian translations. You'll get used to seeing these languages side by side during your time in Switzerland. Everything from supermarket packaging to announcements will be in German, French, and Italian.

The best way to get around Switzerland is definitely with a Swiss Pass. Not only is traveling Switzerland by train incredibly convenient, but it'll also give you stellar views. Train prices, however, can be on the pricey side. That's why many visitors opt for a money-saving rail pass. For example, if you come from Zurich Airport to Interlaken and spend a few days exploring the Bernese Oberland by train before heading back to Zurich, a Swiss Pass will save you big bucks. If you still think it might not be worth getting a Swiss Pass, write down all the trains you're planning to take and look for them in your SBB app. It'll show you the price for each train. This way you can easily add them up and decide if getting a Swiss Pass is worth it or not.

Swiss Pass

If you get the regular Swiss Pass, you can choose between a 3, 4, 8, or 15 consecutive days pass. This allows you to travel Switzerland by train, bus, boat, and even public transport in cities. Some mountain railways and gondolas are not included, but the pass gets you discounts of up to 50%. My favorite thing about the pass is that boat trips are also included. This means you can enjoy unlimited cruises on any lake you desire. In a region like ours, with two stunning lakes, this couldn't be more convenient. Note: This pass is only available for visitors who do not live in Switzerland or Liechtenstein.

Swiss Pass Flex

This pass is almost the same as the regular Swiss Pass, but it allows you to choose your dates beforehand, and they don't have to be consecutive. I always like when train companies offer this option because you'll have more time to explore the region. You can choose from a 3, 4, 8, or 15-day pass. It just depends on your specific itinerary. Note: This pass is only available for visitors who do not live in Switzerland or Liechtenstein.

Half-Fare Card

If you decide against getting the Swiss Pass, the Half-Fare Card is here to save your day (and wallet). Most Swiss people own one since it saves us heaps of money. This particular half-fare card, however, is available for a lower price than us locals can get it and is only available for visitors who do not live in Switzerland or Liechtenstein. As the name suggests, you'll get every train, bus, boat, and public transport ticket for half the fare. Some mountain gondolas and trains are half-price as well but always check beforehand as you don't want to risk a fine. If you don't want to take a lot of train trips on your journey to the Bernese Oberland, this option might be worth looking at.

Cheap train tickets on Omio (formerly called GoEuro)

This app is great because it allows you to buy cheap train tickets in Switzerland. I always check it whenever I have to go somewhere as it's usually way cheaper than buying my ticket at the station. The only catch is that you have to take the exact train you booked. If you miss it, the ticket is no longer valid. With regular SBB tickets, your ticket would be valid for all journeys on the specified route that day.

Before I forget, renting a car is also a convenient way to explore our region. The thing that surprises people the most, however, is that our roads are pretty narrow. If you want to explore all the little villages the Bernese Oberland has to offer, you're going to have to deal with tiny roads. Unless you're comfortable with tight squeezes, I don't recommend renting a car. Anyway, with such a superb public transport system there's really no need to waste valuable vacation time trying to find parking.

6. BEST AREAS TO STAY

One of the most important aspects of your vacation is the place you're based in. For example, when I visited the Italian island of Elba a few years ago, I somehow failed to do any research and ended up staying on the completely wrong side of the island. There was absolutely nothing to do where our hotel was, and we ended up getting a one hour bus every day just to visit the main sights and beaches. I want to make sure nothing like that happens to you, so here's some pre-packaged research to ensure you stay in the best location.

Interlaken and Unterseen

In my opinion, Interlaken and Unterseen are the best vacation bases. Also, if you didn't know they were two separate towns, you probably wouldn't realize. The only thing separating them is the Aare river. Once you've crossed one of the little bridges you're in a different town. Here, you'll be right in the heart of the Bernese Oberland, and every activity and town is no more than thirty minutes away. Stay here if you're looking to thoroughly explore our beautiful region while living right in the midst of it. Personally, I recommend staying in Unterseen rather than Interlaken, since it's quieter and provides even more amazing views of the mountains than Interlaken. You will find several Airbnbs and a few hotels in Unterseen, whereas Interlaken offers everything from budget hostels to luxury five-star hotels.

Grindelwald

This beautiful village is perfect if you want to stay as close to the mountains as possible. You'll have the famous trio of mountains (Eiger, Mönch, and Jungfrau) literally right on your doorstep. If you're looking to head to the Bernese Oberland to go skiing in winter or hiking in summer, Grindelwald is where you want to be. Excursions to the rest of the Bernese

Oberland are obviously still possible, they'll just require a bit more travel time. You'll find Airbnbs, lodges, hostels, and hotels in Grindelwald, so I'm sure there's a place that'll suit your needs.

Thun

If you're more of a city kind of person, Thun may be the place for you. The beautiful old town is fantastic for shopping. You can relax and have a coffee next to the Aare river while you plan your trip through the Bernese Oberland. Thun is a lovely place to base your vacation in if you like living by the lake and want shopping opportunities. From here, you'll be in Bern in only 20 minutes, but the mountains will be a bit further away. Thun offers everything from hostels, Airbnbs, and hotels.

Spiez

This cute village on the shores of Lake Thun will steal your heart as soon as you see it. Spiez, with a castle and vineyards lining the hill around the little bay, is undeniably charming. If you come to the Bernese Oberland in summer, I highly recommend finding a place in Spiez. It'll be a lot quieter than Interlaken. Plus, you'll get to enjoy having the azure lake right in front of your nose. Furthermore, it only takes around 15 to 20 minutes to get to Interlaken, so you're very close to the heart of everything. If you're looking for a more authentic stay in our region, definitely stay in Spiez. (Plus points if you find a place to stay in one of the villages on the way to Interlaken like Faulensee or Leissigen).

Gstaad

If you're looking for a luxury getaway, then Gstaad should be on the top of your list. It boasts everything from luxury hotels to designer shops. Although it's a bit far from the rest of the region, if you're looking for a truly luxurious getaway, Gstaad is the place for you. You can do husky sledding, skiing, and ice skating here in winter, while in summer you can enjoy hiking in the mountains.

7. LUXURIOUS ACCOMMODATION

If you're into luxurious hotels, our region has you covered. Not only do we offer five-star hotels but you can also rent entire Swiss chalets on Airbnb, which will make your trip exceptional. These four are by far the best luxury hotels on offer:

Victoria-Jungfrau in Interlaken

In Interlaken, the fanciest of them all is called the Victoria-Jungfrau Grand Hotel & Spa. It was originally built as the Pension Victoria in 1856. They combined it with the Hotel Jungfrau in 1899, and the Victoria-Jungfrau was born. I've had the pleasure of visiting some of the grand palace-like halls and even some of their rooms. The excellent location in the middle of Interlaken is a bonus.

Le Grand Bellevue in Gstaad

This absolutely beautiful hotel in the resort town of Gstaad is perfect if you're looking for a luxury getaway. Close to ski-lifts and with a wonderful spa, the Grand Bellevue is a hotel that lives up to its five-star reputation.

Dorint Blüemlisalp in Beatenberg

This wonderful four-star hotel in Beatenberg has incredible views over the lake and the surrounding mountains. It's one of the most stunning hotels in our region. Even though it's a bit far from Interlaken, a bus departs every hour and will bring you to town.

Hotel Interlaken in Interlaken

Dating back to the 14th century, this is one of the oldest hotels in Interlaken. It's beautifully renovated, and the food is scrumptious. If you're not staying here, at least treat your taste buds by heading here for a meal.

8. MID-RANGE ACCOMMODATION

Hotels are rather pricey in the Bernese Oberland and finding a decent mid-range one can be tricky. Therefore, I highly recommend picking an Airbnb if your price range falls between luxury and budget. You're spoilt for choice as there are so many exceptional ones dotted around our region. Sometimes, the Airbnbs are in better locations and come with even better views than a hotel in the same town. Airbnbs also gives you the opportunity to stay in little villages that have no hotels. It'll make you feel like a true local.

9. BUDGET ACCOMMODATION

I always enjoy staying in Airbnbs or bed & breakfasts because it feels more personal than hotels. On the other hand, meeting people is a lot easier if you stay in hostels and especially if you're traveling alone. These are my three favorite hostels around Interlaken:

Balmers Hostel in Matten

This is the most famous hostel in the area. It's a charming building with lovely staff and comfy rooms. You'll find lots of cool people to hang out with, whether it's in the hostel itself or the nightclub located underneath. In the nightclub, you'll probably meet lots of locals as well, since it's a favorite among young people from the region. The coolest thing they do happens in summer. You can sleep in tents and teepees as they build an outdoor summer village.

Youthhostel Interlaken in Interlaken

This top-rated hostel is located in Interlaken Ost. The relatively new building offers simple rooms for a reasonable price. Apart from the central location, they also offer fantastic food. Locals even come here to have lunch because the food is so good.

Sonnenhof Interlaken

Situated next to a school and around 20 meters from the Höhematte (the big green field in the middle of Interlaken), the Sonnenhof is perfectly located in the heart of Interlaken. You can get everywhere from here, and travelers give glowing reviews of this hostel.

10. SWITZERLAND ON A BUDGET

Switzerland's not exactly known for being cheap. When you first arrive, everything will look crazy expensive, which is definitely not ideal if you're traveling on a budget. However, it's possible to travel around Switzerland and the Bernese Oberland on a budget. Here's how:

You'll quickly find food is one of the most expensive items you'll need every day. Eating out in restaurants and cafés can take a toll on your wallet. I always like to find myself accommodation that comes with a little kitchen. Head to Migros, one of our biggest supermarket chains, and buy their MBudget products. You'll easily recognize them because of their green packaging with MBudget written in white letters. They're reasonably cheap, and there's only a slight (hardly noticeable unless you grew up with them) difference to the original brand products. Our other big chain Coop has budget-friendly products as well. You will recognize them by the Prix Garantie sign. Although I prefer Migros products, I'll let you decide which one you prefer. Chains like Lidl and Aldi have come to the region as well, and you'll find high-quality products for a cheap price here. Aldi and Lidl are both a bit outside of the center of Interlaken, but if you prefer shopping here, it shouldn't take you too long to walk to one. Cook yourself a nice meal and voilà: You've saved yourself a great deal of money.

Drinking can be costly, so instead of going to a bar, simply buy yourself a couple of beers and chips in a supermarket. Then, head to a pretty place out in nature, by the shores of Lake Thun for example, and enjoy your drinks there! Unlike in America, it's perfectly normal and legal to consume alcoholic drinks outside a bar or restaurant. Also, isn't the lakeside at sunset a much better setting than the inside of a bar? You'll have saved plenty of money and had a nicer evening - two birds with one stone. Just remember to take your empty bottles and trash with you!

When I go grocery shopping, I see many tourists buying lots of plastic water bottles. However, our tap water is not only drinkable but some of the best in the world. You don't need to buy bottles upon bottles of water. Simply refill your own (preferably reusable) with our refreshing tap water. The best thing about that is you'll use less plastic and therefore help the environment.

And the most important thing? Avoid taxis unless you absolutely have to. They are ridiculously expensive. Because public transport is so good, you shouldn't have a problem getting anywhere, so there should be no need to take one. You probably won't see a local ever hailing a cab in your time here.

There's plenty of things to do here for free as well! If you're not up for paying train and gondola tickets, entrance fees, and tour guides, give your wallet a break and choose one of the many free activities the Bernese Oberland has to offer. Interlaken offers a free walking tour for example. A local will guide you around town and show you their favorite spots. But, because I don't want to give all the activities away just yet, I guess you'll have to keep reading.

11. THE CUTEST VILLAGES

Where to start! The Bernese Oberland is full of charming villages. Exploring them is one of my favorite things to do with people who visit. The only things you need are comfortable shoes and a camera to capture your adventures. The best starting point for all of this (as always) is Interlaken, as it's right in the middle of everything.

Iseltwald

Iseltwald is probably the most famous of all of the villages listed here. Who hasn't seen that stunning photo of the castle surrounded by cliffs and the green lake? There are frequent buses here from Interlaken Ost train station. Keen hikers can reach the village from Interlaken by walking along the south shore of Lake Brienz. It's a truly picturesque hike. It doesn't matter what season you choose to go visit. However, the cute Swiss chalets do look better with snow on the roof! Last time I was there, I even saw a traditional wedding party parade through the village.

Beatenberg

Fancy heading to one of the longest villages in Europe? Luckily, it's right around the corner from Interlaken. Take a bus from Interlaken West, which will take you up a windy road until you finally arrive in Beatenberg. The village impresses with a stunning view over Lake Thun and the mountains. Take a stroll through the forest or have a coffee in one of the many restaurants with a view. If you're feeling up for it, you can cycle up here in summer. The road is perfect for pedal enthusiasts.

Wengen

The age-old village of Wengen looks like it's carved into the mountainside. There are no cars in this famous little village, which adds to its bygone vibes. Wengen is especially popular because every year it hosts the famous Lauberhorn Ski Race. Whether you come in winter or summer, Wengen will win you over.

Mürren

This pretty little thing of a mountain village will take your breath away as soon as you set eyes on it. This is especially true in winter when it turns into a snowy wonderland. Whether you head here for a day of skiing or simply to enjoy the scenery (trust me, it's one of a kind), Mürren is an absolute gem.

Gimmelwald

This tiny village lies just a gondola ride away from Mürren. It may be a lot smaller than its famous neighbor, but what it lacks in size it more than makes up for in charm. Gimmelwald is perfect for hiking and taking incredible pictures of the towering mountains that surround the village. I highly recommend stopping here for a quick wander.

Aeschi

This adorable village, which is close to Spiez, boasts amazing views over Lake Thun. It has an even more stunning view over the surrounding mountains. It's a very peaceful and traditional place so just walking around and experiencing the Swissness is well worth it. If you're into cycling, a great trip is from Spiez to Interlaken via Aeschi. Your ride will come with a side of stunning mountain and lake views.

Kandersteg

Even though it's a bit further away from Interlaken, this should certainly make your itinerary. You could, for example, go to Kandersteg on your way to Blausee or Oeschinensee (more on these two lakes later). This charming village is Swiss to the core. Make sure you visit the old church.

12. THE MOUNTAINS AND HOW TO GET TO THEM

The question I get asked the most is how close are the mountains to where I live. The answer? They are super close and easily accessible. You need to get to Interlaken first (unless you decide to base yourself in Grindelwald). From Interlaken Ost, there are frequent trains to Wilderswil, Grindelwald, and Lauterbrunnen - the gateways to the mountains. This depends on which mountain you'd like to go up, of course.

Wilderswil is the first stop on the way to Grindelwald and Lauterbrunnen. If you're going to either of the latter two, make sure you sit in the right part of the train as it splits in half and goes in different directions at Wilderswil. You can also go to Schynige Platte from Wilderswil.

Peaks like Kleine Scheidegg, Männlichen, Jungfraujoch, and First are just a train or gondola ride away if you're in Grindelwald. From Lauterbrunnen, you can head to places like Mürren and the Schilthorn. You can catch the train up to Wengen while a bus will take you from Lauterbrunnen to Stechelberg (where you can reach the Schilthornbahn Gondola).

Once you've decided which mountain you'd like to go to first, look it up in your SBB app and it'll tell you exactly where to go.

13. ICONIC MOUNTAINS TO VISIT

The Bernese Oberland is home to some truly majestic mountains. Here are the most famous ones that are known around the world:

Jungfrau

This famous mountain is home to the Jungfraujoch, which is the highest train station in Europe. And let me tell you, the journey to this 3,454-meter high train station is worth going alone. The train tracks literally go inside the famous north face of the Eiger. Once you reach the summit, you'll have incredible views over the Aletsch Glacier and the Bernese Oberland. You'll also be able to walk through the gorgeous ice palace. If you're on the more adventurous side, you can take your skis, or you can hike to the Mönchsjochhütte, which is around 45 minutes away from the train station (only available from March to mid-October). This is also the starting point for most hiking tours, and you can even sleep here if you fancy. No matter what you do on the summit, going to the top of the Jungfraujoch is a real bucket list experience.

Schilthorn

James Bond fans rejoice! The mountain where they filmed On Her Majesty's Secret Service in 1969 is (obviously) still standing and waiting for you to strike your best Bond pose. It's my go-to mountain when visitors come to Switzerland. Luckily, it's relatively easy to get to this incredibly pretty mountain. The most scenic way to get there is via Lauterbrunnen as right next to the train station is a gondola station that takes you up. Once you arrive at the end of the gondola ride, you'll find a little train station. Hop in and take in the amazing scenery (this is especially nice in winter) as it winds up the mountain to Mürren. After a quick stroll through the cute village, you'll reach the next gondola station, which takes you to the Schilthorn. Before you reach the summit, you'll stop in Birg. I highly recommend getting out to venture along the cliff walk. It's a real highlight as you literally walk on the edge of a mountain on a glass walkway. Seriously cool panoramic views are found here. A little tip for those who don't have a head for heights - don't look down! After you've explored Birg, board the gondola again, and you'll reach Schilthorn in no time at all. Enjoy a meal in the rotating restaurant and wander through the James Bond-themed building. Even the toilets are cool - they play James Bond scenes, and the mirror turns into a screen.

Niederhorn

Niederhorn is the mountain with the big antenna on top. You'll easily spot it, especially at night when it's flashing red. Not only should you admire this stunner from the ground, but you should definitely head up there to enjoy the gorgeous view over Lake Thun and the mountains in the distance. You get great views of the Eiger, Mönch, and Jungfrau (the famous trio) from atop the Niederhorn. The mountain is also perfect for summer hikes as it boasts a seemingly endless amount of trails. The best thing to do here is just to wander around. If you're lucky, you might even see a wild Alpine Ibex. A really popular thing to do here is to get a trottibike and zoom down the mountain. The roads are scenic, and it's a once in a lifetime experience. In winter, Niederhorn is a paradise for sledding and skiing (mostly beginner slopes).

Niesen

We have a saying that states: Hat der Niesen einen Hut, wird das Wetter gut. This means, if the Niesen has a hat, the weather will be good. With a hat, we mean the mountain has clouds shrouding its peak. So, when you spot this pyramid-shaped mountain (trust me you can see it from almost everywhere) wearing a hat you can rejoice because the weather should be nice and sunny. Although I can't vouch for this saying's accuracy, I can with 100% accuracy say that it's a very nice mountain. Whether you hike up or take the really cool funicular, it's definitely worth the trip. The little restaurant on the top serves delicious dishes and stuns with panoramic views over the lakes. Note that the Niesen funicular has a winter break, so do check their webpage to see if the funicular is running or not. It usually opens back up in May. The funicular is only a few meters away from Mülenen train station.

Stockhorn

Not only does this mountain boast a viewing platform, but you can also bungee jump (if you're brave enough) and hike to your heart's content. It's open throughout the year, but the igloo village (unsurprisingly) is only open in winter. It's hard to beat eating a delicious fondue while getting cozy in an igloo. Ice fishing and snowshoeing are also fantastic ways to spend a sunny winter afternoon on the Stockhorn To get here, take the train to Erlenbach station and walk for approximately 10 minutes where you will find the gondola that goes up.

First

Just a quick gondola ride from Grindelwald is First. With activities ranging from a jaw-dropping cliff walk to a scream-inducing zip line ride, First is perfect for the adventurous. The cliff walk not only clings to the side of the mountain; it also boasts a viewing platform that juts 45 meters out into the sky. From the end of the platform, you'll be able to look 2,000 meters down to the valley floor. The zip line zooms across impressive mountain scenery. It's a truly awesome experience! If that's not enough adventure for you, rent trottibikes and speed down the mountain to Grindelwald. In winter, First is an all-time favorite among locals as it offers superb pistes for skiing and snowboarding. In summer, the mountain turns into a hikers paradise, especially the path to Bachalpsee. This stunning lake, which is embedded between mountains, is breathtakingly beautiful.

Harder

Harder is Interlaken's favorite mountain - and not just because the town sits right at its foot! It's a real gem that more than holds its own against the more famous peaks in the region. I suggest taking the funicular one way because it's seriously steep and super cool to ride in. Hiking up is a popular summer activity, but it's also possible in winter - just don't let that snow stop you! But what awaits you at the top of Harder, you ask? Incredible views of Interlaken, Lake

Thun, Lake Brienz, and the Eiger, Mönch, and Jungfrau. The best views are found from the triangular platform that hangs over the edge of the mountain. Note that the funicular doesn't run in winter.

Brienzer Rothorn

If you're in it for the view, Brienzer Rothorn is the mountain for you. Even taking the little red steam train from Brienz to the peak is a highlight. This is also one of my favorite places to brunch because the view is absolutely gorgeous and the food is superb (check the brunch section for more info). From the summit, you're spoilt with interrupted views of mountain peaks and Lake Brienz. It's a top spot for hiking, and you can spend the whole day roaming around up here.

Schynige Platte

A spectacular funicular ride takes you to Schynige Platte. You'll depart from Wilderswil and make your way across scenic Swiss terrain. The train ride (I know I've said this before, but we've got some seriously cool mountain train rides around here) is a real camera-filler. Atop the mountain, you can hike around, have a summer picnic, and soak up the sun.

Note that the train does not run during the winter months.

14. THE MOST STUNNING MOUNTAIN LAKES

Let's talk lakes! Hidden lakes that are tucked away in the mountains are one of my favorite things to see in the Bernese Oberland. The following four are by far the prettiest mountain lakes in the region - and maybe even the world.

Oeschinensee

The gondola station bringing you up to Oeschinensee is easy to reach by train and car. If you're going by train, head to Kandersteg, and from there, you'll have to walk around 15 minutes to the gondola. Back in the day, it used to be an open-air ski-lift gondola that brought you to the lake, and it was one of my favorite things as a kid. Now it's a normal, inclosed-style gondola that transports you to the lake. You'll have to walk down quite a steep path to reach the lake from the station. If you're up for it, you can also hike to the lake from the valley floor. This beautiful turquoise lake, which is surrounded by steep mountain cliffs, is simply breathtaking. In summer, you can go for a swim, but beware as the water is quite chilly. I love taking a backpack full of snacks and drinks as there's no better setting for a picnic than Oeschinensee. Perhaps the best time to visit, however, is winter as the lake turns into one big ice skating rink, and you can even try your hand at ice fishing! Bear in mind you'll have to rent the rods in Kandersteg. It's a true winter wonderland - just remember to wrap up warm.

Blausee

Another equally stunning lake is Blausee, which is just a short drive from Oeschinensee's gondola station. It might not be surrounded by such spectacular mountain scenery, but its magnificent color makes it one of the region's must-visit sites. Blausee translates to Blue Lake in English, and it's by far the bluest lake I've ever seen in my life. The water is so clear that you can see to the bottom of the lake. It's exceptionally beautiful in winter when the blue water clashes with the white snow and ice that surrounds the lake. There's also a fish farm at Blausee, and you can even fish yourself. To get here, go to Kandersteg train station and take a bus to the lake. Try to avoid going here on the weekend as it can be quite crowded.

Bachalpsee

This absolutely stunning lake, just off First, is surrounded by terrain that's perfect for hiking. The lake beautifully reflects the high mountains in front of it and makes for a wonderful view. I found that during the week, the lake is really not that crowded, and you have it almost to yourself.

Aareschlucht

Okay, you got me. This isn't actually a lake, it's a gorge. That doesn't mean it's any less impressive though as this 1.4 kilometer-long gorge between Innertkirchen and Meiringen is a real stunner. You can walk underground and see the Aare river (that you might have spotted running through Interlaken, Unterseen, and Thun) make its way through the impressive gorge. At some points, the gorge gets up to 200 meters deep. I always love visiting here, which is why I included it in this list.

15. WINTER SPORTS

Some of the world's best slopes are located in the Bernese Oberland, but skiing and snowboarding are not the only winter sports available. The region is home to a number of activities that are perfect for the sporty people in your life. But let's start with the classics...

Skiing and snowboarding

There are so many different ski regions to choose from in the Bernese Oberland. The Jungfrau Region's slopes are paradise for beginners and pros alike. When I go skiing, I always try to go on a weekday as the slopes are not as crowded as they are on weekends. My favorite place to ski in this region is at Kleine Scheidegg. Not only do you get fantastic slopes here, but the famous mountains are literally right in front of you. Another top region for skiing is Adelboden. The scenic slopes are some of the best around. I'd encourage beginners to head to Niederhorn as a variety of easy slopes can be found.

Ice skating

Every winter, an outdoor ice rink is built in Interlaken, and there's nothing more magical than skating here. That's probably why it's officially called Ice Magic. It's located in front of the Victoria-Jungfrau Hotel. They play music at night, and there are lots of stands selling food, hot punch, and Glühwein. Another spectacular place for ice skating is on Oeschinensee, a mountain lake near Kandersteg. The lake freezes over in winter, and you can skate on it.

Sledding

If skiing isn't your cup of tea, rent a sled and head up a snowy hill for a fun-filled couple of hours. You can rent sleds almost everywhere. If you want to sled for a really long time though and don't want it to be over in 15 minutes, head to First and walk up to Faulhorn with your little sled. This takes around two hours and is definitely worth it because one of the longest sledding slopes in Switzerland awaits.

Of course, there are numerous other things you can do here, such as ice climbing and snowshoeing. It's best to always go with a guide if you want to partake in ice climbing or wilderness snowshoeing.

16. SKI RACES

We hold several ski races every winter, which range from world-renowned ones to ones for kids and teenagers. They are taken equally seriously! Okay, maybe not equally, but we're a nation that loves skiing. How could we not with the mountains right on our doorstep? If you find yourself here when some of the big races take place, do yourself a favor and join the festivities. These are the two most famous World Cup ski races held in our region:

Ski World Cup Lauberhorn in Wengen
Dates: Usually held in January

The trains to Wengen will be packed, but you might run into some of the skiers participating in the race. The cool thing about this ski race is that when it isn't on, you can ski the exact same slope and pretend to be a professional athlete. The Patrouille Suisse, the air force's aerobatic team, performs a flight show alongside an Airbus from SWISS, our national airline. It's a spectacle that will leave you awestruck as it's not every day you get to see an Airbus flying around mountain scenery.

FIS SKi Adelboden World Cup
Dates: Usually held in January

Join thousands of Swiss ski fans in Adelboden and cheer for your favorite skier. Maybe there's even a skier participating from your home country. No matter who you cheer for, never forget to chant Hopp Schwiiz, which means 'Go Switzerland' when a Swiss skier is zooming down the piste.

17. UNIQUE EXPERIENCES

One of the Bernese Oberland's main selling points is the crazy amount of unique experiences on offer here.

Night sledding
Sledding may not sound too unique. However, you can add a touch of uniqueness to your experience by going on a night sledding tour. It's incredibly fun and really special since the slopes are normally closed at night. Usually, you have fondue in a chalet of sorts before you head down the slopes. While you dunk your bread in molten cheese and enjoy a glass of wine, you can watch it get dark outside. After dinner,

take your sled and head down the mountain with a torch strapped to your head. It's a hit among the locals.

Holzbildhauereischule Brienz

You can take a look around this beautiful wood carving school in Brienz. You'll look over the shoulders of aspiring woodwork professionals for a day. There's also a marvelous exhibit that showcases their excellent wood carving work.

Seilpark Interlaken

There's a climbing park located on the Rugen Hill (where the Rugenbräu beer is brewed), between Interlaken and Wilderswil. I'm usually wary when it comes to things like this, but I have to admit, it's really fun. The Seilpark makes for a fun-filled day for both adults and kids alike.

First Flyer and Trottibike

Ever wanted to zip your way across an 800-meter steel cable at 84 kilometers per hour? Fantastic, because that's exactly what you can do in First. In some places, you're as high as 50 meters above the ground. Afterward, you can speed down the mountain with a trottibike and enjoy marvelous panoramic views.

Make your own chocolate

The Funky Chocolate Club in Interlaken lets you make your own chocolate! Book an hour-long workshop, and you'll be taught how to make the best chocolate bar around. You'll also get to eat as much chocolate as you like. You'll become a true Swiss chocolatier as you learn how to make the perfect bar of Swiss chocolate. All the workshops are held in English, and you'll leave with around 400g of chocolate à la you.

St. Beatus-Höhlen

These beautiful caves in Beatenberg should make your to-visit list. After you arrive at the car park or by bus, the caves are just a short walk away. The walk takes you through lush forest and waterfalls. Once you arrive, you can walk as far as 1000 meters into the mountains. You'll marvel at the stalactites, stalagmites, and beautiful halls as well as hear the story of St. Beatus from one of the guides. The caves are only open from March until October.

Alpine-Slide (Rodeln) Oeschinensee

Oeschinensee doesn't only boast incredibly beautiful scenery, but there's also a really attention-grabbing activity on offer. The alpine-slide is open in summer and provides endless fun. You'll whizz down the mountain for 750 meters on a toboggan track. I remember loving it as a kid, and I still do today.

Fondue in a Hotpot in Brienz

If you like jacuzzis and fondue, this is the activity for you. In winter you can sit in a jacuzzi (while it's hopefully snowing outside) and be served fondue. It's as unique as it's absolutely brilliant! I can't recommend it enough if you're up for something different.

18. SHORT HIKES

It's easy to see why hiking is one of the most popular activities in the Bernese Oberland. Everyone enjoys roaming around the mountains and lakes. Thankfully, you don't need to be a pro hiker to enjoy the walks. Here are a few of the shorter hikes that you can explore around the region:

Harder

Sure, there's a little funicular, but isn't it so much more fun to just enjoy nature and hike up? A friend of mine does this hike almost every two days because she enjoys it so much, and I'm sure you'll love it just as much. The hiking trail starts next to the entrance of the Harder train station, which is a 5-minute walk from Interlaken Ost. From here, the only way is up. Make sure to pack some snacks and drinks. Proper hiking boots aren't necessary, but the hike is just a lot more comfortable with them. After 1.5 to 2 hours (depending on how fast you hike), you'll be greeted with a wonderful view at the summit. Sink a drink or two at the restaurant before stepping onto the triangular platform that hangs over the edge of the mountain for spectacular views of the two lakes and the mountains.

First to Bachalpsee

Make your way to Grindelwald and find the gondola station that takes you to First. Once you're up there, you can start hiking to the beautiful mountain lake of Bachalpsee. This hike can be as long or as short as you want. If you only want to see the lake, it'll take you about an hour to get there from First. You can always extend it by hiking up around

the lake and even back down to Grindelwald. There's
no shortage of things to see around the beautiful lake.
I always love to take a picnic and enjoy the view. The
lake usually mirrors the surrounding mountains,
which makes it even more special.

Bönigen to Giessbachfalls
A little walk by the lake is always nice, but the
hike from Bönigen to the stunning Giessbach
Waterfalls is especially pretty. You'll walk along the
southern shore of Lake Brienz, past Iseltwald, until
you reach the cascading falls. You'll find BBQ
stations dotted along the lake, so bring your own food
and get grilling. You can explore the region around
the waterfalls for as long as you desire as there's a
whole host of things to see and do. If you're still up
for it, you can hike back to Bönigen or take the boat
back, which is an incredibly scenic option. Be sure to
check your body for ticks when you come home as
they are found at the falls.

Leissigen to the Meielisalp (& Suspension bridge)
If you take a train to Leissigen, my home village,
you'll find there's really not that much to do apart
from take photos of the amazing scenery. However,
we do have a restaurant/hotel perched upon a hill high

57

above the village. You can easily hike here. You'll be rewarded with one of the best viewpoints in all the region. You'll have a fantastic view over Lake Thun and the surrounding mountains. After a quick pit stop in the restaurant, head towards the suspension bridge. It's 60 meters tall and 142 meters long and is a real hidden gem for those with a head for heights.

Interlaken- Neuhaus- Beatushöhlen - Merligen
I'm sure you've already read about the famous Beatus Caves. This hike will take you past them, so make room in your busy itinerary and combine this walk with a visit to the caves. You'll start in Interlaken West and hike past the Lombach river toward Neuhaus. Here, you'll walk in the forest in the direction of the popular caves. Next up, walk down to a village called Merligen, which is on the shores of Lake Thun and has lovely views of the region. This whole hike will take you around three hours and 15 minutes, and everything is signposted really well, so you should have no problem.

These are some of my favorite hikes to do in spring and summer. However, there are seemingly millions of other options. Check the Jungfrau

Region's official website for an extensive range of hikes to choose from.

19. LONG HIKES AND CAMPING

If you have a bit more time on your hands and would like to explore our region a bit better, you should opt for one of these longer hikes. There are plenty to choose from, and they can easily be turned into a camping trip. My friends and I thoroughly enjoy camping in the summer. We just pack our things, head up into the mountains, and put our tents up where we like the view. Wild camping is a bit of a weird issue in Switzerland since there are no exact regulations on where you can and can't do it. However, you can't camp in Nature Conservation Areas or (obviously) where there's a sign stating you're not allowed to camp. A lot of farmers allow you to stay on their property if you ask nicely (this is what we do). Just make sure you don't leave anything but footprints behind. Starting a fire is prohibited. However, there are little portable BBQ grills that you can buy in stores like LANDI. This way, you can enjoy your BBQ without accidentally burning a forest down! If you don't fancy camping, but want to spend a night in the mountains, try sleeping in an alpine hut. Locals usually maintain them, and they're staffed throughout the summer. You can sleep in a dorm there for a small fee. They also serve food. Now let's get to the hikes:

Brienzergrat to Harder

This is a rather strenuous hike, but still doable in a day. It's 20 kilometers long and takes you along the mountain peaks of Lake Brienz to Harder. Bring good hiking shoes and inform yourself thoroughly before attempting this hike. If you do feel fit and able enough to do it, you'll be treated with some of the most magnificent views in all of Switzerland. You may even come across an Alpine Ibex. Take the train up to the Brienzer Rothorn early in the morning and start hiking towards Harder. The hike should take around 7 to 9 hours, depending on your fitness.

Morgenberghorn

My personal recommendation is to hike up the Morgenberghorn in two days. On the first day, you should head towards the Brunni, which is a little hut that's serviced by the local ski club in Leissigen. You can sleep in a dorm here. The Brunni is very easy to reach and takes about two hours from either Aeschi or

Leissigen. Everything is signposted, so you should have no trouble finding it. Enjoy the evening in a traditional Swiss hut where you can watch the sunset over the lake and wait for the stars to come out. Trust me when I say it'll be an incredible view! The next morning you can start hiking towards the peak. This hike should take another two hours or so until you reach the top. Enjoy the marvelous view and take fantastic vacation shots before you head back down. Of course, if you wish, you can also do this hike in a day.

For all the hardcore alpine trekkers, I suggest you head to a local tour office where they can recommend the best hike for you. The starting point of the more extreme tours is usually the Mönchsjochhütte. From there you can even climb the Mönch (4,107 meters above sea level) with an experienced, local guide.

20. ADVENTURE ACTIVITIES

Adrenaline junkies tune in! Welcome to adventure central: The Bernese Oberland. I almost don't know where to begin because there are so many adventure-related activities to do here.

Let's start with one of my personal experiences. When I turned 16, my birthday gift was to go paragliding in Lauterbrunnen. At first, I wasn't quite sure how I felt about running off the edge of a mountain with only a parachute and a pilot strapped to my back. I went anyway (face your fears!), and it was one of the greatest experiences of my life. For the first five minutes, I couldn't close my mouth because I was so in awe of everything. I definitely recommend doing this. Your fear will evaporate as soon as you step over the edge as you're flying over one of the most beautiful landscapes in the world.

You can do all sorts of things do get an adrenaline kick here. Whether it's skydiving, bungee jumping, or flying a delta glider, your options are pretty much endless. Water activities, like rafting on the River Lütschine, are also very popular, and rightly so. Even my grandparents have gone rafting when they were younger, and they absolutely loved it. If you fancy going canyoning, you can do it here too.

Outdoor Interlaken is the company you want to turn to if you're looking to do anything adventurous. They organize fantastic tours and activities, no matter what kind of adrenaline junkie you are. Go to their website or visit them in person to find the adventure that suits you best.

Taking a helicopter ride is perhaps the best way to see the Bernese Oberland in all its glory. It's one of the most unique experiences you could do, and the skilled pilots bring you as close to the mountains as possible. If you want to surprise someone special, this is definitely the way to do it.

21. SPAS

Traveling is exhausting in a very good way. Sometimes you just need a few hours to relax and recharge your batteries (I know I do). Thankfully, our beautiful region doesn't disappoint. If you can, be sure to make time in your busy sightseeing itinerary between coffees and mountain hikes to head to a spa and relax.

Beatus Spa in Merligen
The Beatus Spa sits right on the lake and has an outdoor thermal pool. I love sitting in the pool in the depths of winter and being nice and warm as the snow

falls. Be sure to treat yourself to one of the massages and treatments and enjoy the beautiful saunas.

Victoria-Jungfrau Spa in Interlaken
The Victoria-Jungfrau in Interlaken offers a truly luxurious spa, including private treatments, steam baths, massages, warm pools, and saunas.

Bödeli Bad in Interlaken
Interlaken's local swimming pool is also a spa. In summer, it's great just to go swimming in their outdoor pools, while in winter, their sauna will keep you nice and toasty. Another plus point is that it's much more affordable than the previous two.

Hammam Spa in Bern
So, Bern isn't technically in the Bernese Oberland, but our lovely capital is probably already somewhere on your busy travel list. When you visit, pay a trip to my absolute favorite spa. You don't even have to take swimwear as you'll get a towel to wrap around yourself. It's a very special and unique spa in an absolutely beautiful setting.

22. SCENIC DRIVES

Roads that line lakes and wind up mountains are in ample supply in the Bernese Oberland. So rent a bike or car and just cruise around the area to soak in the epic views that are found on our road network. If you don't want to get behind the wheel, it's still possible to experience some of the most scenic routes on public transport.

Interlaken to Thun

My absolute favorite is known as the Bucht - or 'the bay' in English. The Bucht is the drive between Interlaken and Thun along the north shore of Lake Thun. The cliff-hugging road is a delight to drive. You can get a fantastic view of it when you're on a boat on Lake Thun.

Interlaken to Grindelwald

You'll go past incredible mountain scenery and see the mountains appear closer and closer. The ability to stop everywhere and take pictures of everything is definitely a bonus if you're traveling in a car to Grindelwald.

Interlaken to Beatenberg

Whether it's in your own car or by bus, this windy road produces fantastic views of Lake Thun. Once you reach Beatenberg, the views get even more dramatic. Stop at the Luegibrüggli restaurant for a coffee - it's a great boost at any time of the day.

Interlaken to Lucerne

The drive from Interlaken to Lucerne goes via the Brünig pass, and that's definitely something that should be on your list. You'll drive along Lake Brienz before heading up the pass. Windy roads lead up the mountain and give you stunning views of waterfalls and jaw-dropping alpine landscape.

Grimsel Pass

This pass connects Haslital (part of the Bernese Oberland) with the Canton Valais. It's an incredibly scenic drive. You'll even see a painting of Melisande on the dam of a reservoir lake. This drive is especially popular amongst bikers and is only open during the summer months.

23. SCENIC TRAINS

Who said train journeys are boring? In Switzerland, you won't want the ride to end as so many of our tracks cut through dramatic alpine landscapes. You'll fill your camera before you even arrive at your destination!

Wilderswil to Kleine Scheidegg

Nothing says Switzerland more than snowy mountains outside a train window. If you head from Wilderswil up to Kleine Scheidegg, you'll be in awe of how close the train gets to the famous mountains. Also, the trains have extra big windows so you can see better - and take uninterrupted photographs.

Kleine Scheidegg to Jungfraujoch

The journey to the highest train station in Europe goes behind the famous north face of the Eiger to provide you with stunning mountain views.

Interlaken to Bern

The short journey from Interlaken to Bern runs along Lake Thun and gives you amazing vistas and countless opportunities to take photos. On the approach to Bern, you'll get the most stunning view of the city as you glide over a bridge.

Interlaken to Lucerne
Venture into another canton! The train ride from Interlaken to Lucerne glides by the shores of Lake Brienz and up the Brünig pass. You'll continue to wind through a dreamy landscape of lakes and mountains until you reach the picture-perfect city of Lucerne. It's a true Swiss experience.

Wilderswil to Schynige Platte
This train literally clings to the edge of a mountain as it takes you to the summit of Schynige Platte. Incredible panoramic views await you on top as well as during the ride up.

24. WATERFALLS

If you're anything like me, the prospect of seeing waterfalls will excite you. Luckily, we have some spectacular ones in our region, and here are the best of the best:

Reichenbach Falls

I assume you've heard of Sherlock Holmes? One of the books in Sir Arthur Conan Doyle's series is called Reichenbach Falls. It's quite famous among fans of the quirky detective. I'm not sure how accurate to reality the book is, but I do know that Reichenbach Falls is an actual (and awesome) place in the Bernese Oberland. As well as the beautiful scenery, it's well worth checking out to discover where Sir Arthur Conan Doyle got the inspiration for his famous book.

Trümmelbach

These beautiful falls in Lauterbrunnen are super scenic. The waterfalls crash down into caves, and you can walk very close to many of the different falls in the caves. Be sure to walk underground and overground so to see the fabulous waterfalls from different angles. It's definitely a unique spot for waterfall-lovers.

Giessbach Falls

A bit closer to Interlaken, you'll find one of my favorite waterfalls. If you have the time, you should save an entire day for these falls. Take a backpack and fill it with things you can easily put on a BBQ.

To get started, go to Interlaken Ost or Bönigen and hop on a boat that'll take you right to the Giessbach Falls. After you finished exploring this beautiful area, head towards the hiking trail that goes along Lake Brienz. Here, you'll find several little BBQ stations where you can sit and roast your sausages. Just remember to bring a lighter!

Staubbach Falls

Probably the most famous of them all is the Staubbach Falls in Lauterbrunnen. You can see them from almost everywhere in Lauterbrunnen as they drop a spectacular 297 meters over the edge of a cliff. Maybe you'll even see one or two base jumpers as Lauterbrunnen is the capital of this (somewhat crazy) sport.

25. WILDLIFE

In terms of wildlife, we don't have a whole lot to offer. However, what we do have is still well worth trying to see. Keep an eye out for the chamois (which is a species of goat-antelope) that roam our mountains. If you look down below when you're on a ski lift, you might see them running about. A bit closer to Interlaken, I've seen them climbing around on Harder from a friends balcony. We call them Gemschi.

We also have deer, squirrels, and foxes in our woods, but I highly doubt you'll see any of them since they're very shy. Alpine marmots, or Murmeli, call our mountains home as well. They are quite adorable, but they're also very shy, so the chance that you'll see one in the wild is quite low. Maybe you can hear one whistle as they whistle when they sense danger before vanishing into their holes in the ground.

Our most famous animal, however, is the Steinbock (also called the Alpine Ibex). If you're lucky, you might encounter one during a hike. Some of my friends have seen them on the Brienzergrat (see longer hikes). They have impressive, curved horns and look pretty majestic. Don't go too close to them as you wouldn't want to be attacked (and possibly thrown off a mountain) by one of those guys. Enjoy them from a distance.

26. LAKE THUN AND LAKE BRIENZ

Ah, the lakes! What would Interlaken be without the two picturesque lakes at either end of the town? Because I grew up on Lake Thun, I might be quite biased when I say it's my favorite of the two, but you'll have to decide for yourself which one you prefer. It's too close to call for many locals and visitors. Here's what you can do:

Rollerblade from Leissigen to Faulensee

If you can get your hands on some rollerblades or a bicycle, head to the very end of Leissigen (about 10 minutes from the train station), and start a very scenic journey along Lake Thun to Faulensee.

Bike around either lake

Locals love biking around either of the lakes. You should be able to do it in around a day if you're reasonably fit and like to stop now and then to admire the view. You can rent a bike from several places in Interlaken.

Hop on a boat

There's nothing better than exploring our lovely lakes by boat. In summer, when we're not in a rush, locals love taking boats instead of the train because it's just much more scenic and relaxing. The most beautiful boats on the lake are the paddle steamers. There's one on each lake. Make sure you catch the Lötschberg on Lake Brienz and the Blüemlisalp on Lake Thun for an authentic experience.

Watch the sunset in Neuhaus

Trust me when I say this is the best spot in our region to watch spellbinding summer sunsets. The sun sets in just the right place, so it illuminates the water. You can rent pedalos, paddleboards, and kayaks here. In the evening, use one of the public BBQs for the perfect end to a dreamy summer's day. Getting here is easy as well, simply hop on a bus in Interlaken that's heading in the direction of Sundlauenen and get off at Neuhaus.

Ride the jet boat on Lake Brienz

Are you up for an adrenaline-pumping adventure on Lake Brienz? Book a seat on the jet boat that runs from mid-April to mid-September and enjoy a crazy ride! With 360 degree turns, this thrilling ride is the perfect summer activity for thrillseekers.

27. WATERSPORTS

There are so many amazing things to do on and under the lakes that it's hard to pick a favorite activity.

In summer, one of the best ways to relax after a long day is to rent a paddleboard in Neuhaus and paddle out into the lake to watch the sunset unfold. When the sun starts to set, you'll be in the right place to see the water turn into liquid gold.

Another of my summer favorites is found at Bönigen on Lake Brienz. Here, you can rent a kayak and paddle around the lake. Be sure to dock in the beautiful village of Iseltwald!

Guess what? You can even go diving here. Although Lake Thun doesn't boast coral reefs and colorful fish, exploring the underwater world is still great fun. Head to the Dive Center Thunersee in Hilterfingen to rent some gear.

Wakeboarding and waterskiing are also two popular summer activities. You can book trips at Mountainsurf in Interlaken or at the Wakeboard School in Gunten. And, even if you've never tried it, it's great fun and makes any sunny day a bit more exciting and adventurous.

Surfing is not the first activity that springs to mind when you think of Switzerland, but you can go river surfing in Thun. You'll probably spot a surfer or two riding the wave on the river Aare in summer and even in winter (brrrr).

28. SPECIAL EVENTS

It's highly likely that you'll encounter a special event during your time in the Bernese Oberland as we have so many of them. From rock concerts to yodeling festivals, here are some of the best:

National Day
Let's start with our National Day on August 1st. It's one of the two times a year where you don't need special permission (welcome to Switzerland) to set off your own fireworks. The other occasion being New Year's Eve. Throughout the day and night of August 1st, you'll hear and see them going off all over the place. The most spectacular display in the Bernese Oberland takes place on the Höhematte,

which is in front of the Victoria-Jungfrau Hotel. As well as the fireworks, the crowds at the Höhematte get to witness a massive bonfire.

New Year

Funnily enough, Interlaken doesn't celebrate the New Year with fireworks and a concert on December 31st. We do it on January 1st. Like I said, the Swiss like to be different! The 'Touch the Mountains' event takes place every January 1st and consists of a concert followed by a firework display.

Harderpotschete in Interlaken

If you want to learn more about the myth surrounding the Harder mountain, you should turn to the 'Legends' section in this book. Long story short: On January 2nd, Interlaken celebrates something called the Harderpotschete. People don scary wooden masks and parade through town to get rid of evil spirits. It's been running for almost fifty years, and if you happen to be around on January 2nd, you shouldn't miss this totally unique parade.

Seenachtsfest Spiez

One of the loveliest celebrations we have is called the Seenachtsfest, which translates to 'Lake Night

Party.' It's usually held sometime in July. However, the dates change every year so you should check beforehand. Concerts, soccer games, and an impressive show from the Patrouille Suisse (the Swiss Air Forces' aerobatic team) take place. The night ends with spectacular fireworks.

Brienz Yodelling Festival

No, not every Swiss person can yodel. But during the Yodelling Festival in Brienz, you can hear the pros yodel their hearts out. Soak in the traditional atmosphere as Brienz is transformed into a little yodeling village in June. You'll also be able to watch people partake in Fahnenschwingen, which is essentially incredibly skilled people throwing around flags. It's a lot cooler than it sounds.

Oberländisches Schwingfest in Interlaken

In summer, Interlaken gears up to display Schwingen, our age-old national sport. It's a type of wrestling that's quite fun to watch. You'll see people dressed up in traditional Swiss outfits and probably hear the alphorn, which is our national instrument. It's about as Swiss as it gets.

Jungfrau-Marathon

Sometimes dubbed the most beautiful marathon in the world, the Jungfrau-Marathon is a real hit with runners from around the world. The participants have to tackle a 42 km course that climbs an astonishing 1,829 meters. The incredible course starts in Interlaken and finishes at the foot of the Eiger Glacier. It's a spectacle that locals love to watch, and if you're here in September, join the cheering crowds or (if you're slightly crazy) sign up for the race.

Trucker & Country Festival in Interlaken

Since the early 1990s, this annual festival has brought trucks and bikers from all over Europe to Interlaken. It's all about country music and showing off your vehicle. Put on your cowboy hat because you'll definitely look out of place without one. As the dates vary every year, check their webpage to find out when it takes places this summer.

Thunfest

Thun also has its own little festival every year. Usually, they hold it for a few days in August, and the whole city is in celebration. Food stands, carousels, and concerts make Thun a fantastic place to visit during the festival.

Unspunnenfest in Interlaken

So this one is rather rare. Every 12 years Interlaken hosts the Unspunnenfest, which is a traditional festival where you'll see Swiss wrestlers and traditional costumes worn around town as well as alphorn players. The highlight is a lot of strong people throwing a very heavy stone to see who throws it the furthest. It sounds rather strange, but it's great fun to watch.

Greenfield

A hard rock festival is maybe not the first thing that comes to mind when you think of Interlaken. Yet people from all over Europe come to Interlaken every summer to see world famous rock and heavy metal bands. Musicians like Green Day, Linkin Park, and the Foo Fighters have played this stage before. If you're here during the festival, you might even be able to hear the bands play without having to buy a ticket. Trust me, Interlaken gets quite loud.

29. CHRISTMAS MARKETS

Visit the Bernese Oberland in December, and you'll be met with illuminated houses, the occasional Samichlaus (Santa Claus) strolling with a donkey by his side, and LOTS of Christmas markets. Be sure to put on your warmest clothes and head to one of the many Christmas markets to try all of these treats.

Nidletäfeli

Make sure to try the fudge that we call Nidletäfeli. Bonus points if you can order them in Swiss German. They are absolutely delicious - very sweet though. For me, they taste like Christmas.

Glühwein

A classic. How better to warm up on a cold winter's night than with mulled wine? Usually, it's red wine, but a little stand at the Interlaken Christmas market sells white mulled wine, and it's delicious. After a few of them, you might be able to order them in German (Glühwein). After a few more, you might even have the confidence to order one in Swiss German (Glüewi).

Punch (Apple, orange, and rum)

If alcohol isn't your thing, you don't have to freeze through the night as punch is here to save you from the cold. It's what I drink when I walk through Christmas markets. You can get apple, orange, or rum flavored punch at almost every Glühwein and food stand. If you find a stand that sells hot apple juice with cinnamon you hit the jackpot. It's my favorite winter drink! I always make it at home, so if you can't find a stand, buy a bottle of cloudy apple juice and a bit of cinnamon and boil it.

Magenbrot

Magenbrot, a kind of gingerbread cookie, should also be enjoyed at least once. Magenbrot translates to 'stomach bread,' which is quite an odd name, but it's said to be good for digestion. If you're a fan of gingerbread, you'll be a fan of Magenbrot, for sure. It's a whole lot sweeter than gingerbread though.

Brönnti Mandle

Brönnti Mandle are caramelized almonds. If you can get your hands on these, make sure to hide them from everyone else since they tend to disappear in about 10 seconds. They're that tasty!

Marroni

You'll find marroni stands everywhere as roasted
chestnuts are the best chestnuts. Throughout winter,
you can find my favorite one, which is still painted
the same as it was in 1998. You can find it by the big
crossing on Bahnhofstrasse in Interlaken. They make
for a tasty snack while you explore Interlaken on foot.

30. SPORT

There are plenty of sports on offer that don't
involve going up a mountain and zooming down a
piste. What these sports lack in altitude, they more
than make up for in atmosphere, scenery, and
facilities.

Football

If you're into football, I have great news for you as
Interlaken is home to one of the prettiest pitches in
the world. The mountain-lined ground is really close
to Interlaken Ost and serves as FC Interlaken's home
pitch. Many locals go here for a kickabout, and I'm
sure you're more than welcome to join them. I've
even lost a few games here. If you're looking to
watch a professional team, head to the Stockhorn

Arena in Thun. This modern arena holds 10,000 people and plays host to FC Thun.

Tennis Courts

You may have heard that one of the best tennis players of all time comes from Switzerland, so we honor him by putting up tennis courts just in case he ever swings by. Just kidding, but we do have several fantastic courts - especially in the Bernese Oberland. The clay courts on the Höhematte in Interlaken are certainly some of the best I've ever seen.

Ice Hockey

Ice hockey is big in Switzerland. The fast-paced games are fun to watch (if you can keep your eye on the puck!), and the lively atmosphere makes for a great occasion. You can go and watch SC Unterseen-Interlaken play. However, down the road in the capital is SC Bern, who are one of the biggest clubs in Europe.

Basketball

You can play basketball at the Gymnasium (High School) in Interlaken. The courts are usually empty, and you can play for however long you want. Just bring your own basketball.

31. WHERE TO TAKE THE BEST PHOTOS

It's very hard to take a bad photo in our region. Your photos are sure to make everyone at home envious! I love wandering around the region and stumbling upon secret spots. Luckily, you're holding the perfect guide in your hands that'll point you straight to the locations that should end up in your photo album.

Harder, Interlaken

Harder is known as Interlaken's house mountain. It's super easy to reach, and the summit's triangular platform (which hangs over the edge of the mountain) provides breathtaking vistas of the Swiss Alps, Lake Brienz, and Lake Thun. There's no better place to see Interlaken and the lakes. Whether you hike up or take the funicular (which runs from April to December), you'll find an incredible location for snaps.

Birg

Sure, you'll get great shots from atop the Schilthorn, but the most amazing photos are at Birg, the station before the summit. Here, you'll find a famous cliff walk that provides an unbeatable setting for truly amazing mountain photography. The cliff walkway looks like it's glued to the edge of the mountain. If the glass floor doesn't get your heart racing the tightrope (don't worry, there's sturdy netting underneath) certainly will. Be sure to come here in winter so you can snap the Alps in all their snowy glory.

Iseltwald

Iseltwald has long been a favorite with locals. In recent years, however, the village's popularity has soared thanks to social media. People come from far and wide to recreate the famous snap of the village's castle-like building that juts out into Lake Brienz.

Oeschinensee

This place is perfect for that unique Swiss vacation shot. The spectacular lake is great for photos in winter (when it's frozen over) and in summer (with its bright green color). It doesn't matter where you go to snap the perfect picture as Oeschinensee looks great from every angle. The high mountains surrounding it make for a truly spectacular scenery that you have to include in your album.

Aeschi

Aeschi is a cuter-than-cute little town that's located in the hills above Lake Thun. Thanks to its elevated location, you can photograph the famous wolkenmeer, which is a sea of clouds. On a cloudy day, you have a chance to be above the clouds. You can also see this phenomenon when you're skiing, but I think it's especially beautiful from Aeschi.

Wengen and Mürren

Look no further than Wengen and Mürren if you're looking for picture-perfect Swiss villages to explore. During wintertime there's almost always heaps of snow here, so you can fill your camera with snow angels as well as beautiful snaps of the snow-capped chalets. On top of going on a photo walk, some of Switzerland's best ski slopes are found near the two villages.

Leissigen Pier, Lake Thun

In my hometown of Leissigen, there's a little pier that stretches into Lake Thun. It makes for great pictures of the lake and surrounding mountains, especially at sunset. If you arrive by train, walk to the lakefront, and you'll see the pier running adjacent to the church.

Neuhaus, Lake Thun

Neuhaus (and the surrounding area) is a ridiculously pretty park on the banks of Lake Thun. Your Instagram won't be complete without a picture here - preferably on a stand up paddleboard or pedalo. This is a top spot for romantic sunset photos.

Waterfalls

Whether it's the Giessbachfalls or the famous Staubbachfall in Lauterbrunnen, there must be at least one waterfall included in your photo album. The challenge here is to not getting your camera wet while capturing that perfect shot.

32. WHERE TO GET ARTSY

Our entire region should be considered art, but apart from that fact, there are a few specific places where you can admire art and music.

Kunsthaus in Interlaken

Interlaken's Kunsthaus holds frequent art exhibitions. In summer, they also put on free outdoor concerts. The Kunsthaus is right in the middle of

Interlaken. It'll take you around 10-15 minutes to get there from either train station.

Ballenberg between Brienz and Brünig

This open-air museum takes you back in time. It displays how people lived in Switzerland back in the day. You can even participate in some of the exhibitions. The musical among you can play some of the historical instruments, while the crafty can create their own toy. It's super interesting for people of all ages, and I love taking visitors here. I like to combine it with a peaceful boat trip to Brienz followed by a bus to the stations of either Ballenberg East or West.

Tellspiele in Matten

If you want to see amateur actors reenact the legend of Wilhelm Tell in an open-air theater, then the Tellspiele in Matten is the place for you. The actors are locals - some of my friends even participated. Real horses and authentic costumes help bring the show to life. The arena is right next to Matten's big ice rink, and you can easily walk there from Interlaken. This is only seasonal as it's an open-air theater, so check if it's on when you're visiting.

33. WHERE TO GO FOR RETAIL THERAPY

You won't find a plethora of big brands in the Bernese Oberland. There's an H&M in Thun, and that's about it. For other high street shops, like Zara or Mango, you'll have to head to nearby Bern. While this might be annoying at times, it also gives you the opportunity to support local businesses.

Because I travel so much, I get the chance to shop in different cities around the globe. Yet, one of my favorite shopping streets to stroll through is the picturesque Bälliz in Thun. Trains and buses connect Thun with Interlaken. Trains will get you there a lot quicker than buses, but the bus follows a more scenic route along Lake Thun (which I mentioned in scenic drives).

Gstaad is the place to go if you're looking for luxury shops. It gives St. Moritz a run for its money. I definitely recommend going there, even if it's just to wander the streets and people watch.

Grindelwald, on the other hand, is more relaxed and sells mostly ski gear and souvenirs. It's lovely

walking through the streets with the towering
mountains in the background.

34. SOUVENIRS TO BRING BACK

I always love bringing souvenirs to my family
from all the destinations I've visited. Sometimes, it
can be tough to choose between the countless options
you're presented with. I usually aim for something
that doesn't end up in a corner collecting dust. Here
are three things your loved ones will either find useful
or just absolutely delicious.

Eigerspitzli
There will be a lot of disappointed faces awaiting
you at home if you don't bring back a bar or two of
Swiss chocolate. But do you really want to give them
some Toblerone or Lindt? You can buy them
anywhere in the world! Instead, opt for some
Eigerspitzli. These lovely chocolates are shaped like
the Eiger. They even have a white top to resemble the
snow at the summit of the famed mountain. These
gems are created in the Jungfraujoch Confectionary,
which at 2,322 meters above sea level, is Europe's

highest-altitude confectionary. Either you get your hands on a packet of these delicious little treats here or from the LANDI store in Interlaken if you don't fancy a trip up the mountain.

Mondaine Railway watches

Everyone loves Swiss watches, so what better gift to give than a timepiece you actually bought in Switzerland? Contrary to popular belief, you don't have to sell your house to purchase one as there are quite a few brands that sell affordable yet high-quality watches. The most popular one being the Mondaine Railway watches. They have the same design as the clock in the railway stations and make for a fantastic souvenir.

Swiss army knife

I'm always asked if I carry a Swiss army knife, and I have to disappoint as I don't actually own one. My family has plenty though, and they're super handy in a whole number of situations. I always borrow one if I'm heading to the lake for a BBQ. Every time I use one I promise to buy myself one as they're amazing.

35. FOODS YOU HAVE TO TRY

Swiss cuisine has a lot more to offer than just fondue and raclette. As you already know about the classics, I'm going to skip them and dive straight to the things you simply have to try.

Chips

If, like me, you're a fan of chips, you'll love being in Switzerland as, in my opinion, we make some of the best in the world. What Switzerland's chip industry lacks in variety of flavors, it makes up for in taste. Our two basic flavors are salt and paprika. Somehow we didn't quite get the memo on quirky chip concoctions like prawn cocktail or flame grilled steak. My personal favorites are the Snacketti Shells, and the kangaroo-shaped chips from Chio called Jumpys. Be sure to keep an eye out for them as they make for the perfect snack.

Fish from the Fischerei Sieber in Leissigen

Fish is not the first thing that comes to mind when you think of Swiss food. But here's a secret tip that should make it to the top of your list: If you want the freshest fish in all the region, head to my hometown, Leissigen. Our red crest has two white fish on it for a reason! Getting here is quite simple as it only takes 10-15 minutes by train or car from Interlaken. If you're on foot, it'll take around 15 minutes to walk there from Leissigen (some bits are by the busy main road). In the little store of Fischerei Sieber, you'll find several different types of freshly caught fish and even some chicken and quail eggs. Be sure to pick up some trout (Seeforelle) and perch (Egli). You can get them smoked (warm or cold). Communication with the local fisherman might not be easy (unless his daughter's home) since he doesn't speak much English. However, with a little bit of pointing and a smile, I'm sure you'll receive the fish you wanted.

Rösti

You'll find lots of places that dish up mouthwatering Röstis in the Bernese Oberland. You're also in luck if you want to create one at home as they're quite easy to make. Most Rösti recipes tell you to cook the potatoes first. My family's secret tip, however, is to put the potatoes in the pan raw. The taste is a lot fresher that way.

Räubereggechueche

Unterseen is home to a cute bakery called Michel Beck. Not only do they sell delicious croissants, but they also serve a unique dessert. It's called Räubereggechueche (good luck pronouncing that!). You'll find Michel Beck on Scheidgasse street. However, the street used to be called Räuberegge (which means robber's corner) and the bakery named a delicious cake after the old street.

Älplermacaroni
This hearty dish is one of my favorite Swiss meals. Translated, it means macaroni from the Alps. It's made with a whole lot of cheese, potatoes, and cream, and is then baked to perfection. It's absolutely delicious. You usually find it in restaurants close to or on ski slopes.

Ovomaltine products
Ovomaltine products are a real favorite among the Swiss. You'll find their products in major supermarkets - and I recommend you try as many of them as possible, especially their crunchy chocolate spread and cookies.

36. WHERE TO FIND THE BEST SWISS FOOD

To tell you the truth, the best Swiss food is found at my grandparent's place. Unfortunately, they haven't opened their kitchen to the world just yet, so you'll have to settle for one of these traditional restaurants until they do.

Taverne in Interlaken

This restaurant is located inside the ancient Hotel Interlaken. Their menu offers a wide selection of delicious Swiss food, but they're most famous for their fondue. Head here for a truly cheesy experience.

Bären in Unterseen

If you want to try an authentic Swiss Rösti, then Bären in Unterseen is the place to go. The cute Swiss interior is just a bonus to the fantastic food they serve. They also offer a hunger-quenching brunch.

Chemihütte in Aeschi

Chemihütte, situated in the little village of Aeschi, is well worth a visit. As well as serving super tasty Swiss food, the restaurant also comes with panoramic views of Lake Thun, so it's easy to see why it's incredibly popular with locals. Go here to experience true Swiss food that's cooked with love.

37. A HANDY GUIDE FOR CHOCOHOLICS

You've certainly come to the right place if you're looking to try some of the best chocolate in the world. Our streets are practically paved in chocolate. Okay, not quite, but basically every store in the region sells tasty treats. With so much choice, it can be hard to find the best, most delicious chocolate. However, there are three that stand above the rest.

Läderach

You'll find this classy chain of shops all around Switzerland, including Interlaken high street (close to Interlaken West station). The chocolate is hand-made, and even their shop window will make your mouth water. They have a vast assortment of pralines and unique chocolate creations. If you're looking for authentic Swiss chocolate to sink your teeth into, then you can't go wrong with Läderach.

Schuh

Schuh is located opposite the Metropole hotel. Besides being a cute café that serves taste bud tantalizing desserts, it's also a confectionary that puts on chocolate shows. Quirky creations (such as a shoe or a Santa Claus) made entirely out of chocolate can be bought or simply admired in the shop window. Definitely head here for exceptional chocolate in unexpected shapes.

Eigerspitzli

These lovely little treats are crafted in Europe's highest confectionary. The chocolates resemble the famous Eiger mountain, and the tip is dunked in a white sugarcoat to look like snow. Get your hands on some of these on your trip to the Jungfraujoch, or if you don't fancy traveling all the way up there, you can find them in the LANDI in Interlaken.

38. BEST BRUNCH PLACES

There's only one thing better than brunch, and that's a brunch with a beautiful view! Luckily we have plenty of brunch spots that come with a side of mountain vistas. Here are four of the best:

Brienzer Rothorn

Enjoy a unique brunch while marveling at one of the most ridiculously beautiful views in all of Switzerland. To get to the Brienzer Rothorn, you'll have to head to Brienz where you catch a red funicular up the mountain. It's an incredibly scenic train ride. Once you've reached the summit, a delicious brunch can be found in the restaurant. Also, after brunch, you can explore the region on foot and hike to secluded spots with even better views. Happy exploring!

Victoria-Jungfrau

The five-star Victoria-Jungfrau offers an incredibly tasty brunch. In fact, everything you've ever wished for in a brunch buffet comes true here! Make sure to book a table in advance and also to arrive with an empty stomach as this brunch is a real belt-buster. In summer, I recommend reserving a table in the garden underneath the grapevines as you'll get to enjoy a great view of the mountains. There's an entire meat and fish grill section as well as a chocolate fountain and all the traditional breakfast food you can imagine. A glass of champagne is also included, so what are you waiting for? Treat yourself to an incredible brunch in this stunning five-star hotel.

Schilthorn

You can tuck into this brunch all year round, but the views are at their best in winter. I mean, you can't really beat looking out over mountains covered in snow, can you? The brunch in the rotating panoramic restaurant on top of the mountain is as unique as it is delicious. And the best part? After brunch, you'll get to enjoy a whole day of skiing through the region.

Restaurant Alpen Tower

Another place that offers a great brunch with stellar views is the Restaurant Alpen Tower. Perched high in the Swiss Alps, this beauty spot is best reached from Meiringen where a scenic gondola ride will quickly transport you to the mountains. After a hearty brunch, spend the afternoon exploring the incredible scenery.

39. BEST CAFÉS

It's super hard to find the perfect café when you're visiting somewhere for the first time. To avoid mediocre coffee and unfriendly atmospheres in the Bernese Oberland, simply head to these lovely spots.

Café de Paris in Interlaken

The Café de Paris is located in the heart of Interlaken and is my personal favorite. It's where I go to have coffee with my friends and talk about what's going on in our lives. They serve great cocktails and nice hot chocolates as well as snacks, meals, and desserts in a lovely, homely atmosphere.

Velo Café in Interlaken

Velo Café is a charming café that's hidden in an alley in the center of Interlaken. Velo means bicycle in Swiss German, and you'll find actual bikes hung up all over the place in this café.

It's super cute and has a great selection of coffee and tea. It's close to the Amman-Hofer Platz and relatively easy to find. Also, at the back of the café is a drawer filled with board games, which is a fun way to pass the time on a particularly rainy day.

Altstadt Teehaus in Unterseen

Right by the Stadthausplatz in Unterseen is an adorable café called Altstadt Teehaus, which you may have guessed means old town tea house. It lives up to its name as you can find loads of delicious tea varieties here. It doesn't matter which one you end up going for as they all taste amazing. Anyone who likes tea will love this little gem of a café.

40. BEST RESTAURANTS

When you're visiting a new destination, the question is always: Where will we eat lunch? Where's good for dinner? Instead of having to look through hundreds of restaurants on TripAdvisor, I suggest you go with one of my recommendations.

Café de Paris in Interlaken
I know I listed this as one of my favorite cafés, but they also serve top notch meals to satisfy a range of tastes. I like to go here with my friends for a casual lunch or afternoon drinks with a snack. Their salads are exceptional, and the wraps are equally delicious.

Appaloosa in Spiez
This adorable restaurant in Spiez offers delicious Tex Mex food. The fajitas are especially tasty. The atmosphere is friendly and inviting while the interior is super cool. It's a favorite among locals, and I

always love eating there. It's great for a fun night out with friends.

West End in Interlaken
If you're looking for the best Italian food in the region, look no further than the West End in Interlaken. It serves the most delicious Italian food around. It's located right next to the big Migros store in Interlaken West, so it's easy to find. My personal tip is the saffron risotto - it's the best I've ever had.

Meielisalp in Leissigen
Definitely go here if you're up for having lunch with a view. Head to Leissigen and drive (or walk) up the windy road that leads to the Meielisalp. This lovely hotel also has a restaurant where you can enjoy lunch with a picture-postcard view over Lake Thun. It's especially beautiful in summer as you can combine lunch with a walk over the suspension bridge that's just a short hike away.

OX in Interlaken
Located right next to Café de Paris is OX. Here, you can enjoy some of the best meat dishes our region has to offer in a unique environment as cow bells hang above your head. This traditional yet stylish

restaurant is not only nice to look at, but the food is also fantastic. Be sure to try one of the burgers as they're absolutely delicious.

Luegibrüggli in Unterseen/Beatenberg
Another restaurant with an exceptional view over the area and Lake Thun is the Luegibrüggli. It's located on the edge of a rugged cliff between Unterseen and Beatenberg. You can either take a car there or the bus to Beatenberg, and it'll stop right outside the restaurant. It doesn't only serve lovely food but stuns with panoramic views of the lake and surrounding mountains.

El Azteca in Interlaken
This cute Mexican restaurant in the heart of Interlaken doesn't only offer a stylish interior but also yummy authentic Mexican food and a wide range of tequilas. Because almost everything here is made from cornflour, people with gluten or lactose intolerances can eat almost anything. My tip for an unforgettable night? Order the surprise menu and get six delicious dishes to munch your way through.

Han in Thun

This Mongolian BBQ restaurant is one of my absolute favorites for special occasions or just a fun night out. Pick up a plate and put as many raw ingredients on it as you want. Chicken, seafood, and a variety of vegetables are all on offer. You hand your plate to a chef who will then cook it right in front of your eyes. Add sauces and spices and enjoy your dish. You can go back to the buffet as many times as you like and it's absolutely exquisite.

41. THE BEST ICE CREAM IN THE WORLD

Ask any local from Interlaken where you'll find the best ice cream, and they'll all (in unison) tell you to go to Gelateria Azzurra immediately.

It doesn't matter what season you come to Interlaken. Whether it's freezing cold or meltingly hot, you simply have to try the best ice cream in the world. Trust me on this, I've tried many ice creams around the globe, and none have lived up to what you can get from Gelateria Azzurra in Interlaken. You'll find pure happiness in the form of ice cream here.

The hand-made ice cream comes in a wide variety of flavors, including seasonal ones such as chestnut (marroni) and cinnamon. There's even a rice flavored one! After trying all of them over and over again, I concluded that the cookie ice cream is the best of the best. It's a bonus the people running it are super friendly and will help you with any questions you may have regarding their ice cream.

42. TASTY DESSERTS AND WHERE TO FIND THEM

This is for all the sweet-tooths out there. There are so many dessert options in the Bernese Oberland that it can be tough to decide what to stick your spoon into first. Worry not as I'm here to guide you through the best of the best.

Café de Paris in Interlaken
Unsurprisingly, my favorite café, the Café de Paris, makes it onto the list. You can find my number one dessert on their menu. It's called Öpfelchüechli, which means little apple cakes. These little fried apple cakes are dunked in cinnamon sugar and served

with warm vanilla cream, (the best) cinnamon ice cream, and fresh fruit. If this doesn't make you want to run there right now, then I don't know what will.

Bäckerei Wüthrich in Grindelwald

This lovely bakery in Grindelwald offers not only tasty bread but also a great selection of desserts. You can even buy chocolate that's made by the bakery. It looks beautiful and tastes even better. Another specialty of theirs is the St. Martinsringli cookie, which has a hole in it as it's based on the legend of St. Martin. According to the legend, there was a lake behind Mettenberg mountain, and if the lake became blocked with ice, it would overflow and drown animals and locals. To stop this from happening, the people prayed, and St. Martin came down from the heavens and moved the mountain a little to prevent the disaster. When he saved the day, he left a hole in the mountain, which you can still see the sunshine through today. The butter almond cookies of the bakery have a hole too, and they're really delicious.

Confiserie Rieder in Interlaken

Right opposite the Café de Paris is Confiserie Rieder. Besides a tasty brunch and a great hot chocolate, you'll find some of the best desserts in the

region. Take your pick from one of the many cakes
and enjoy the lovely interior of this café. The staff are
super friendly and will gladly help you choose the
best cake for you. It's a tricky decision!

hairatelier&bistro in Gsteigwiler
Next up is this adorable little bistro in the tiny
village of Gsteigwiler. It might seem a bit off the grid,
but that's what makes it so charming. You can board
a bus in Interlaken West, and 15 minutes later you'll
find yourself marveling at the Eiger, Monch, Jungfrau
from this remote village. As well as admiring the
incredible view of the always snowy mountains,
you'll be able to enjoy a tasty dessert in one of my
favorite cafes, hairatelier&bistro (yes, it's also a hair
salon!). Definitely come here if you want to eat
fantastic, 100% home-made desserts in one of the
most Swiss villages around.

Bäckerei Konditorei Steiniger in Matten
Not only does this bakery make amazing bread
(seriously, try it!), they also serve delicious desserts.
Choose one or two of the many little desserts
displayed in their window and eat it inside or as a
takeaway. I always like to pick up a little sweet treat
and eat it on the go, but the choice is yours.

43. DRINKS YOU HAVE TO TRY AND HOW TO ORDER THEM

We have quite a few local and unique drinks that you have to try while you're in the Bernese Oberland.

Rugenbräu

We brew our own beer in the Bernese Oberland. It's called Rugenbräu, and it's created in a little brewery on a hill called, you guessed it, Rugen. If you're a beer lover, you can't leave the region without sampling a few bottles. Also, if you want to impress the local bartender, try to order a beer the Swiss way, which goes as follows: Order a Stange if you want a 3dl beer. If you order a Herrgöttli, you'll get 2dl of beer. Finally, if you'd like to have your beer mixed with Sprite, order a Panache.

Hugo

You'll find this popular drink on menus all over Austria, Germany, and Switzerland. I suggest you head to your nearest bar and order one because they're incredibly refreshing. It's made with prosecco, elderflower syrup, and sparkling water. Mint leaves are added for decoration.

Ovomaltine/Caotina

The best thing to drink when you enter a restaurant from the wintery outdoors is a steaming mug of hot chocolate. You'll be presented with two options in Switzerland: Ovomaltine or Caotina. Here's the thing, everyone in Switzerland has a favorite (mine changes every week). Try both of them and decide which one you like best. Also, this is not only a great drink in winter, but you can also have cold Ovomaltine or Caotina in summer. Both are very refreshing.

Rivella

It only occurred to me when I was about 7 years old that Rivella was something you could only get in Switzerland. I vividly remember being very upset when I couldn't order one in the south of France! Rivella may sound a little odd as it's made with milk (well, milk serum to be precise) and looks like beer (without the foam), but it's one of the most popular drinks in Switzerland. It has a very unique taste, and there are three different versions: Rivella Red, Rivella Blue, and Rivella Green. Every Swiss person has their favorite version with Rivella Green somehow being the least popular. My favorite is blue. Find your favorite by tasting all three and by the end of your trip, you'll be as sad as 7-year-old me when you realize you can't have it in your home country.

Wine from Spiez

Remember Spiez, the beautiful town on Lake Thun? The hills are lined with vineyards, and thankfully the wine is for sale. Most of the restaurants in Spiez serve the local wine. For the best experience, I recommend heading to a restaurant or bar in Spiez that overlooks the bay and enjoy one or two glasses of wine. Alternatively, try a few glasses while soaking in the scenery on a vineyard tour.

Flauder

Another soft drink you need to try is Flauder. The fizzy drink is infused with flowery alpine tastes such as Melissa balm and elderberries. You can get several different variations, and I suggest you try all of them.

44. BARS AND NIGHTLIFE

The Bernese Oberland isn't exactly the nightlife capital of Switzerland, but we do have a few bars and nightclubs that make for a fun evening. Here's where to go when you're thirsty:

Hüsi Bierhaus in Interlaken

If you want to have drinks in a laid back atmosphere, Hüsi is definitely the place to head to. It's a popular spot for both locals and visitors due to their special craft beers and fruit beers - the latter being my personal favorite.

The 3 Tells Irish Pub in Matten

This proper Irish pub is located in the middle of Matten and is easy to reach by foot from the center of Interlaken. The fish n' chips are the thing to order on the menu - as is a pint of Guinness (or two).

Brasserie in Interlaken

This little gem of a bar should be on everyone's Interlaken itinerary. They serve flavorful beers and a wide selection of drinks in a lovely atmosphere. No visit is complete without trying their ribs and chicken wings as they're the best in town!

Las Rocas in Interlaken

This Latino Bar is right in the heart of Interlaken. It welcomes visitors with a stylish interior and refreshing cocktails. Their guacamole and nachos are also a delicious add-on. It's one of the best spots to relax after a long day of sightseeing.

Balmers Club in Interlaken

If you're up for a club night, then this is where you'll find a proper Swiss night out. Located underneath the famous Balmers Hostel, you'll find many backpackers and locals throwing some moves on the dancefloor.

Hangover in Interlaken

Two locals opened up this lively nightclub near Interlaken West station in 2018. You're guaranteed great drinks, cool music, and most probably a hangover!

Aprés-Ski

You'll find Aprés-Skis across the region. It's the name given to open-air bars in the mountains that you go to after a long day of skiing. You listen to Schlager music and enjoy a drink or two. Hot drinks infused with alcohol (like coffee with schnapps) are a particular favorite of locals.

45. LEGENDS

Every place has its legends - and the Bernese Oberland is no different. Here are three of the most famous found in Interlaken and Switzerland in general.

The Hardermannli

If you find yourself in Interlaken, you can't fail to see the Harder mountain. You can hike up there (see day trip hikes) and get stunning views over the whole area. But there's also something hidden in the mountain. We call it the Man of the Harder (Hardermannli) as the rocks are aligned to look like the face of a man with a big black mustache. If you can spot it without asking a local for help or googling it, then you're one step closer to becoming a local. Legend has it that in the 16th century there was a young girl from Ringgenberg (a village close to Leissigen) who liked going to church. There was a man, nicknamed Harder, who chased her and she fell to death from the mountain. God apparently damned the man and had him forever carved into the mountainside. Every January 2nd, Interlaken is full of people that dress up as the Hardermannli in an attempt to rid evil spirits. Drums and music accompany them as they parade through Interlaken in their funny costumes.

Wilhelm Tell

Though it's not set in the Bernese Oberland, this famous legend is known by everyone in Switzerland. The story of our national hero (though fictional) is of a peasant who was forced to shoot an apple from his son's head with a crossbow because he offended the Austrian leader, Gessler. Get to know the rest of the iconic story by visiting the Tellspiele in Matten. It's performed by local actors every summer in an open-air theater.

St. Beatus

If you visit the St. Beatus Caves in Beatenberg, you'll have to know the legend that took place there. The monk, St. Beatus, took refuge in the caves but to his displeasure, he discovered there was already something living there. The horrible dragon didn't like the intruder and angrily spat fire at St. Beatus. The old monk stood his ground and fought the dragon until the creature tumbled down the cliff and into Lake Thun. Visit the beautiful caves and see if you can find remnants of the epic battle between the monk and the dragon.

46. DON'T FREAK OUT IF YOU SEE...

I definitely don't want you to be freaked out by something that's considered normal in the Bernese Oberland. Therefore, I've created a little list of oddities that you may encounter during your time in the region.

Loud jets cruising around

You're more than likely to see military jets in the skies. This is normal and absolutely nothing to worry about. I only realized this was weird when I worked in Interlaken. I was on the phone with a client and had my window open just as the jets thundered past. The person on the other line was pretty shocked and asked me if everything was okay. The Bernese Oberland is a great place for the military to train its pilots. One of their airports is in Meiringen, near Brienz. The airfield is easy to reach by car, and you can even watch the jets take off.

Decorated Cows

Yes, you read that correctly! If you visit in spring or fall, you might witness an Alpaufzug or an Alpabzug. In spring, farmers decorate their cows with flowers and special bells and parade them through town before walking up the alp with them. The cows spend all summer living their best life before being walked down in fall. So, if you're trying to go grocery shopping and twenty cows are walking down the street - don't worry, that's totally normal.

A sky full of paragliders

Throughout the year, the skies above Interlaken and Lauterbrunnen are practically covered with paragliders, delta gliders, and other such adrenaline junkies. It's quite a pretty sight and also completely normal. You didn't just walk into a paragliding festival. Also, if you hear random screams coming from the skies, it's usually them having a good time.

Military men

Military service is mandatory for Swiss men, and they're automatically enrolled aged 18. There are a few perks that come with the service. Namely, your loved ones can send you free letters and packages (usually filled with food!), and if you're in your military uniform, you can ride on public transport for free. It's common to see a soldier in full uniform heading home on the train. They sometimes have their rifles with them although they never carry ammunition.

Cows everywhere

If you go hiking in the Alps in summer, there will be cows chilling in fenced areas. Sometimes, however, the hiking trail goes through the fenced area. This means you'll have to open the fence, enter the 'cow area,' and hike through the field. Be careful where you step though! At the end, there will be another gate where you can exit the field. Make sure to always close the gate after leaving.

Closed shops

Most shops close on Sundays, especially grocery stores. This is due to a law in Switzerland that prohibits certain industries staying open on Sundays. Interlaken has the privilege of being a tourist hub. Therefore, our stores get special permission to stay open on Sundays so you'll have no issues buying groceries.

47. MYTH BUSTING

There are a lot of myths out there about life in Switzerland, so I thought I'd clear up some of the more famous ones so you can experience the Bernese Oberland like a local.

No noise after 10 PM

For my birthday, my best friend gave me a scratch map of the world. On the back, were tips on what to do and not do in some countries. For Switzerland, it said that it's illegal to flush the toilet after 10 PM. Sounds quite horrifying! I'm happy to report that's not true. I can see how the scratch match creators got such an idea as you generally shouldn't be making too much noise after 10 PM. This includes loud music, hammering nails, etc. It's not illegal per se, but if you have a picky neighbor, they would be entitled to call the police. Don't worry, you won't be arrested, they'll just politely ask you to stop. This also applies for lunch hours (12 PM-1 PM) and all day Sunday. I had to learn this the hard way when I hoovered my apartment at 12.30 PM and got a complaint letter. I agree with the rule to some extent, but even I thought that went a little too far!

Keep your lights on

If you rent a car or motorbike in Switzerland, remember to always have the lights on - even in broad daylight. It's illegal to drive with your lights off, and if the police stop you, you might be fined. According to studies, accidents are a lot less likely to happen with lights on, so it makes sense to do it.

Washing schedules

If you live in an apartment block (or rent an Airbnb in one), there's something you need to know about washing machines. First of all, it's very rare for a Swiss apartment to have its own washing machine; they're usually found in the cellar or basement. Most apartment blocks have a monthly schedule with a timetable where you can write your name to secure a slot (e.g., wash from 8 AM-10 AM on Thursday). One of the big no-go's is to leave in your washing in the machine after your time slot finishes. You'll get in big trouble with the neighbors. Also, coming back to rule number one, do not use it after 10 PM or on Sundays.

What does CH stand for?

You'll see CH crop up time and time again when you're in Switzerland. Plenty of cars have a CH sticker, our web domain is .ch, and our currency is even abbreviated to CHF. So what does the CH mean? It's an abbreviation for Confederatio Helvetica (the Helvetic Confederation), which is the Latin name for Switzerland.

President(s)

Usually, countries have one representative, a president for example. Switzerland likes to be different, as always. We don't just have one head of state; we have seven. Seven!

Three kisses

In some countries, you greet a friend with a kiss on either cheek. In other countries, a firm handshake is the norm, while a hug is the go-to greeting in loads of places. In Switzerland, we give three kisses on the cheek (left-right-left) to say hello to a friend.

48. WHAT EVEN IS SWISS GERMAN?

Unless you have a keen interest in obscure languages, you probably don't understand how Swiss German works. A common misconception is that we simply speak German with a bit of an accent. A lot of people think of it like British English and American English. Surprisingly, even a lot of Germans that I've met think this, and yet when they visit Switzerland, they hardly understand a word we're saying! Even though it technically is the same language, Swiss German is essentially a very strong, distorted dialect.

Here's an example to see how it works. If (for some reason) you'd like to tell someone you ate a carrot it would sound like this:

Swiss German
I ha es rüebli gässe.

German
Ich habe eine Karotte gegessen.

English
I ate a carrot.

You see, they're completely different! A German speaker would really struggle to understand what a Swiss person is talking about. With other sentences, however, you can clearly tell the languages are related. Take the below sentence as an example. A

121

German speaker is likely to understand what a Swiss person is talking about. They're almost identical, but with a slightly different pronunciation.

Swiss German
Das isch mir no nie passiert!

German
Das ist mir noch nie passiert!

English
That never happened to me!

We use Swiss German to talk, text, and post on social media, but there are no written rules. All of our school books, newspapers, and literature, however, is in German (or High German as we call it in Switzerland). Our TV channels are mostly from Germany and therefore in High German. However, there are two Swiss channels, SRF1 and SRF2, so if you'd like to hear some Swiss German (and occasionally some Romansh), tune in and check it out.

To add to the confusion, each canton has its own accent, which makes it even harder for foreigners to

understand. In the canton of Bern, we speak
Bärndütsch (Bern German), while our neighboring
canton, Wallis, speaks Walliserdütsch (Wallis
German). Most of the time, we understand each other
quite well. However, a lot of cantons have a hard time
understanding people from Wallis. It's like a Scot
speaking to someone from England. They understand
each other fine - just some words and phrases cause
confusion.

People from the canton of Bern, including those
from the Bernese Oberland, are famous for speaking
with a very slow accent. If you listen to locals talk to
each other, you might realize that some of them really
do speak quite slowly and like to stretch words out.

It's always nice to impress the locals with a bit of
Swiss German. Maybe you've heard of Grüezi and
know it stands for hello/good day. That's correct.
However, it's only used in certain cantons like Zurich
and Lucerne. In Bern, you won't be very popular if
you go up to someone and say that. As you know
now, every canton likes to be a bit different, and in
Bern, you say Grüessech.

Here's some (random) slang that you'll only ever hear in Bern. Every time I use one of these words with friends from other cantons, I get weird looks and/or laughs.

Küder   Means 'trashcan'. Other cantons say 'Abfall'.

Himmelgüegeli   Means 'ladybird'. Other cantons call it 'Maiechäferli'.

Äuä   Means 'No way!' or 'I guess'. Other cantons don't have this word and even struggle with pronouncing and using it correctly. It's probably our most famous word. If you say you're from Bern, someone will eventually mention 'Äuä' to you.

Äcke   Means 'neck'. Other cantons call it 'Nacke'.

Anke   Means 'butter'. Other cantons simply say 'Butter'.

Hudel/Hudu   Means 'cloth'. Other cantons call it 'Lumpe'.

Chätschi   Means 'chewing gum'. Other cantons say 'Kaugummi'.

As you can see, some words are completely different depending on what canton you're visiting. Even us Swiss sometimes struggle to communicate within our own country. Luckily enough there's High German to fall back on if we don't know what the other person means. And by the way, you'll be absolutely fine speaking High German to everyone you meet in the Bernese Oberland.

49. USEFUL PHRASES IN SWISS GERMAN AND GERMAN

Now that you understand how Swiss German works, here's a little list of useful phrases you might need during your stay in the Bernese Oberland. This will certainly impress the locals as well as help you in certain situations, like when you really need a beer!

English Swiss German German
Thank you! Merci! Dankeschön!
You're welcome. Isch gern gsche! Gern geschehen.
Yes please. Ja bitte. Ja bitte.
How are you? Wi geits? Wie geht's?
No thank you. Nei danke. Nein danke.
Have a good day! Schöne Tag! Einen schönen Tag!

125

Where's the bathroom? Wo isch z'WC?   Wo ist die Toilette?

Could I have a beer? Chönnti es Bier ha? Könnte ich ein Bier haben?

Do you speak English? Redet dir Englisch? Sprechen Sie Englisch?

Can I see the menu? Chönnti z'Menü gse? Könnte ich das Menü sehen?

Help! Hilfe! Hilfe!

I need help. I bruche Hilf. Ich brauche Hilfe.

Where is the hospital? Wo isch ds Spital? Wo ist das Spital?

This is beautiful. Das isch schön. Das ist schön.

Can I pay? Chönnti zahle? Könnte ich zahlen?

Where is this? Wo isch das? Wo ist das?

Could you show me? Chönntet ihr mirs zeige? Könntet Ihr es mir zeigen?

Cheers! Proscht! Prost!

50. DO'S AND DON'TS

Either you've finished the book (yay!), or just skipped to this chapter to see a quick summary of all the do's and don'ts, which is definitely something I would do - just don't tell anyone! Anyway, here's a quick summary on the do's and don'ts of Switzerland and the Bernese Oberland.

Do

• Have a chat with the locals - they'll appreciate it.

• Whip out some of your newly acquired Swiss German.

• Ask for help if you need it. Swiss people don't usually come up and offer help since they don't want to intrude, but they're happy to help if you ask.

• Wave thanks to cars that let you cross a road. Every Swiss person does this.

• Remember that trains are always on time so don't be late!

• Switch off your mobile data, especially if you're from the EU.

• Greet your friends with three kisses on the cheek.

- Shake someone's hand if you're meeting them for the first time.
- Say Proscht when you cheers! Touch glasses with everyone and look each other in the eye.

Don't
- Call a Swiss person German or Swedish. We're proud of being Swiss.
- Jaywalk. Rules are rules, you know?
- Get on public transport without a ticket unless you want a hefty fine.
- Be late!
- Spit on the ground as it's considered very rude.
- Cross or walk on train tracks.
- Ask for salt and pepper if it's not already on the table. It insults the chef's cooking.
- Leave your trash lying around. There are bins everywhere - use them!
- Make loud noise after 10 PM. We're very strict on that one.

TOP REASONS TO BOOK THIS TRIP

Jaw-dropping scenery

The Bernese Oberland is one of the most beautiful regions in the world. Its breathtaking scenery includes snow-capped mountains, alpine lakes, and cascading waterfalls.

Memory-making activities

There's a wide range of adventurous experiences and laid-back activities to enjoy. Whether you're kayaking on an alpine lake or skydiving over the Swiss Alps, you'll never be bored here.

Perfect weather

There's never a bad time to visit. Summer is ready-made for hiking in the mountains and swimming in the lakes while winter travelers get to explore a snowy wonderland.

OTHER RESOURCES:

https://www.myswitzerland.com/en-id/home.html (Switzerland's official tourism)

www.sbb.ch   (Railway)

https://www.swiss-pass.ch (Swiss Pass)

https://www.omio.com (Omio Train Tickets)

https://www.jungfrau.ch (Official page of the Jungfrau Region)

https://schilthorn.ch/en/welcome (Schilthorn)

https://www.niederhorn.ch (Niederhorn)

https://www.niesen.ch (Niesen)

https://stockhorn.ch (Stockhorn)

https://brienz-rothorn-bahn.ch/?lang=en (Brienzer Rothorn)

https://www.oeschinensee.ch/en/ (Oeschinensee)

https://www.interlaken.ch/en/discover-interlaken.html (Interlaken's Official Webpage)

https://www.outdoor-interlaken.ch/en (Outdoor Interlaken)

Photo Suggestion (Royalty Free from Unsplash)
A lovely picture of the Jungfraujoch
https://unsplash.com/photos/OwbelFfiuUk

PACKING AND PLANNING TIPS

A Week before Leaving

- Arrange for someone to take care of pets and water plants.

- Email and Print important Documents.

- Get Visa and vaccines if needed.

- Check for travel warnings.

- Stop mail and newspaper.

- Notify Credit Card companies where you are going.

- Passports and photo identification is up to date.

- Pay bills.

- Copy important items and download travel Apps.

- Start collecting small bills for tips.

- Have post office hold mail while you are away.

- Check weather for the week.

- Car inspected, oil is changed, and tires have the correct pressure.

- Check airline luggage restrictions.

- Download Apps needed for your trip.

Right Before Leaving

- Contact bank and credit cards to tell them your location.

- Clean out refrigerator.

- Empty garbage cans.

- Lock windows.

- Make sure you have the proper identification with you.

- Bring cash for tips.

- Remember travel documents.

- Lock door behind you.

- Remember wallet.

- Unplug items in house and pack chargers.

- Change your thermostat settings.

- Charge electronics, and prepare camera memory cards.

READ OTHER
GREATER THAN A TOURIST
BOOKS

Greater Than a Tourist- Geneva Switzerland: 50 Travel Tips from a Local by Amalia Kartika

Greater Than a Tourist- St. Croix US Birgin Islands USA: 50 Travel Tips from a Local by Tracy Birdsall

Greater Than a Tourist- San Juan Puerto Rico: 50 Travel Tips from a Local by Melissa Tait

Greater Than a Tourist – Lake George Area New York USA: 50 Travel Tips from a Local by Janine Hirschklau

Greater Than a Tourist – Monterey California United States: 50 Travel Tips from a Local by Katie Begley

Greater Than a Tourist – Chanai Crete Greece: 50 Travel Tips from a Local by Dimitra Papagrigoraki

Greater Than a Tourist – The Garden Route Western Cape Province South Africa: 50 Travel Tips from a Local by Li-Anne McGregor van Aardt

Greater Than a Tourist – Sevilla Andalusia Spain: 50 Travel Tips from a Local by Gabi Gazon

Children's Book: *Charlie the Cavalier Travels the World* by Lisa Rusczyk

135

> TOURIST

Visit *Greater Than a Tourist* for Free Travel Tips
http://GreaterThanATourist.com

Sign up for the *Greater Than a Tourist* Newsletter for discount days, new books, and travel information:
http://eepurl.com/cxspyf

Follow us on Facebook for tips, images, and ideas:
https://www.facebook.com/GreaterThanATourist

Follow us on Pinterest for travel tips and ideas:
http://pinterest.com/GreaterThanATourist

Follow us on Instagram for beautiful travel images:
http://Instagram.com/GreaterThanATourist

Follow *Greater Than a Tourist* on Amazon.

.

> TOURIST

At *Greater Than a Tourist,* we love to share travel tips with you. How did we do? What guidance do you have for how we can give you better advice for your next trip? Please send your feedback to GreaterThanaTourist@gmail.com as we continue to improve the series. We appreciate your constructive feedback. Thank you.

METRIC CONVERSIONS

TEMPERATURE

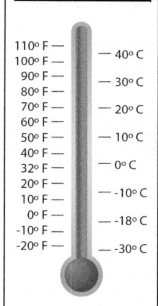

110° F —	— 40° C
100° F —	
90° F —	— 30° C
80° F —	
70° F —	— 20° C
60° F —	
50° F —	— 10° C
40° F —	
32° F —	— 0° C
20° F —	
10° F —	— -10° C
0° F —	
-10° F —	— -18° C
-20° F —	— -30° C

To convert F to C:
Subtract 32, and then multiply by 5/9 or .5555.

To Convert C to F:
Multiply by 1.8 and then add 32.

32F = 0C

LIQUID VOLUME

To Convert:.................Multiply by	
U.S. Gallons to Liters................	3.8
U.S. Liters to Gallons	26
Imperial Gallons to U.S. Gallons	1.2
Imperial Gallons to Liters.......	4.55
Liters to Imperial Gallons	22

1 Liter = .26 U.S. Gallon
1 U.S. Gallon = 3.8 Liters

DISTANCE

To convert ....Multiply by	
Inches to Centimeters	2.54
Centimeters to Inches	39
Feet to Meters......................	.3
Meters to Feet	3.28
Yards to Meters	91
Meters to Yards	1.09
Miles to Kilometers	1.61
Kilometers to Miles............	.62

1 Mile = 1.6 km
1 km = .62 Miles

WEIGHT

1 Ounce	= .28 Grams
1 Pound	= .4555 Kilograms
1 Gram	= .04 Ounce
1 Kilogram	= 2.2 Pounds

141

TRAVEL QUESTIONS

- Do you bring presents home to family or friends after a vacation?

- Do you get motion sick?

- Do you have a favorite billboard?

- Do you know what to do if there is a flat tire?

- Do you like a sun roof open?

- Do you like to eat in the car?

- Do you like to wear sun glasses in the car?

- Do you like toppings on your ice cream?

- Do you use public bathrooms?

- Did you bring your cell phone and does it have power?

- Do you have a form of identification with you?

- Have you ever been pulled over by a cop?

- Have you ever given money to a stranger on a road trip?

- Have you ever taken a road trip with animals?

- Have you ever went on a vacation alone?

- Have you ever run out of gas?

143

- If you could move to any place in the world, where would it be?

- If you could travel anywhere in the world, where would you travel?

- If you could travel in any vehicle, which one would it be?

- If you had three things to wish for from a magic genie, what would they be?

- If you have a driver's license, how many times did it take you to pass the test?

- What are you the most afraid of on vacation?

- What do you want to get away from the most when you are on vacation?

- What foods smells bad to you?

- What item do you bring on ever trip with you away from home?

- What makes you sleepy?

- What song would you love to hear on the radio when you're cruising on the highway?

- What travel job would you want the least?

- What will you miss most while you are away from home?

- What is something you always wanted to try?

- What is the best road side attraction that you ever saw?

- What is the farthest distance you ever biked?

- What is the farthest distance you ever walked?

- What is the weirdest thing you needed to buy while on vacation?

- What is your favorite candy?

- What is your favorite color car?

- What is your favorite family vacation?

- What is your favorite food?

- What is your favorite gas station drink or food?

- What is your favorite license plate design?

- What is your favorite restaurant?

- What is your favorite smell?

- What is your favorite song?

- What is your favorite sound that nature makes?

- What is your favorite thing to bring home from a vacation?

- What is your favorite vacation with friends?

- What is your favorite way to relax?

- Where is the farthest place you ever traveled in a car?

- Where is the farthest place you ever went North, South, East and West?

- Where is your favorite place in the world?

- Who is your favorite singer?

- Who taught you how to drive?

- Who will you miss the most while you are away?

- Who if the first person you will contact when you get to your destination?

- Who brought you on your first vacation?

- Who likes to travel the most in your life?

- Would you rather be hot or cold?

- Would you rather drive above, below, or at the speed limited?

- Would you rather drive on a highway or a back road?

- Would you rather go on a train or a boat?

- Would you rather go to the beach or the woods?

TRAVEL BUCKET LIST

1.

2.

3.

4.

5.

6.

7.

8.

9.

10.

Printed in Great Britain
by Amazon

20382607R00092